The Nellie Massacre of 1983

The Nellie Massacre of 1983

The Nellie Massacre of 1983

Agency of Rioters

Makiko Kimura

SAGE STUDIES ON INDIA'S NORTH EAST

$SAGE www.sagepublications.com
Los Angeles • London • New Delhi • Singapore • Washington DC

First published in 2013 by

SAGE Publications
B1/I-1 Mohan Cooperative Industrial Area
Mathura Road, New Delhi 110 0⁴
www.sagepub.in

SAGE Publications Inc
2455 Teller Road
Thousand Oaks, California 91320, USA

SAGE Publications Ltd
1 Oliver's Yard, 55 City Road
London EC1Y 1SP, United Kingdom

SAGE Publications Asia-Pacific Pte Ltd
33 Pekin Street
#02-01 Far East Square
Singapore 048763

Published by Vivek Mehra for SAGE Publications
10/12pt Adobe Garamond Pro by RECTO Graphics, Delhi and printed at Saurabh Printers Pvt Ltd.

Library of Congress Cataloging-in-Publication Data Available

ISBN: 978-81-321-1166-5 (HB)

The SAGE Team: Rudra Narayan, Dhurjjati Sarma, Anju Saxena, and Rajinder Kaur

Cover photograph: Painting *Immortal Bliss* by Pranab Baruah. Photograph of the painting by Anjuman Ara Begum.

To the survivors of the Nellie massacre

Thank you for choosing a SAGE product! If you have any comment, observation or feedback, I would like to personally hear from you. Please write to me at contactceo@sagepub.in

—Vivek Mehra, Managing Director and CEO,
SAGE Publications India Pvt Ltd,

Bulk Sales

SAGE India offers special discounts for purchase of books in bulk. We also make available special imprints and excerpts from our books on demand.

For orders and enquiries, write to us at

Marketing Department
SAGE Publications India Pvt Ltd
B1/I-1, Mohan Cooperative Industrial Area
Mathura Road, Post Bag 7
New Delhi 110044, India
E-mail us at marketing@sagepub.in

Get to know more about SAGE, be invited to SAGE events, get on our mailing list. Write today to marketing@sagepub.in

This book is also available as an e-book.

———————✵❀✵———————

Contents

List of Illustrations

Tables

Figures

Maps

List of Abbreviations

AAGSP	All Assam Gana Sangram Parishad
AAMSU	All Assam Minority Students' Union
AASU	All Assam Students' Union
ADSF	Autonomy Demand Struggling Forum
AGP	Asom Gana Parishad
ASS	Asam Sahitya Sabha
ATSU	All Tiwa Students' Union
AUDF	Assam United Democratic Front
BJP	Bharatiya Janata Party
CPI	Communist Party of India
CPI (M)	Communist Party of India (Marxist)
CRPF	Central Reserve Police Force
GOI	Government of India
GUTA	Gauhati University Teachers' Association
IAS	Indian Administrative Service
IDP	Internally Displaced Person
LAC	Lalung Autonomous Council
PGR	Professional Grazing Reserve
PLP	Purbanchaliya Lok Parishad
PTCA	Plains Tribal Council of Assam
RSS	Rashtriya Swayamsevak Sangh
ULFA	United Liberation Front of Asom
UPF	United People's Front

Acknowledgments

I visited Nellie for the first time in 2001 to do fieldwork for my PhD research on the antiforeigner movement in Assam. I wanted to learn about how indigenous peoples (tribes) had participated in the movement and a friend suggested that I visit Nellie, where indigenous peoples had joined the movement and lent a hand in attacking Muslims in 1983. At the time, I did not have much of an idea about the Nellie incident. I knew that an attack had taken place there, but I never imagined it to be one of the largest cases of mass killings in contemporary India. I had no idea then that I would visit Nellie and central Assam (Morigaon and Nagaon Districts) time and time again, and then write a book on the incident.

The reason I continued working on the Nellie incident and the issue of collective violence in India was perhaps because I could not fully understand how "ordinary people" in peaceful villages around Nellie could take part in the killings. Why do people participate in killing their neighbors? And how do they live with those memories? My search for answers to such questions is what led me to write this book, which is an attempt to answer these queries.

Many people supported and helped me while I researched the antiforeigner movement and the Nellie incident. At the outset, I would like to thank Professor Tiplut Nongbri of Jawaharlal Nehru University, who supervised my PhD research on Assam's antiforeigner movement. I am grateful to the examiners of my thesis, Professor Virginius Xaxa of the Tata Institute of Social Sciences (Guwahati campus) and Professor Monirul Hussain of Gauhati University. Their comments were greatly beneficial to me as I began reworking the manuscript of this book. It was a great joy to interact with Professor Sanjib Baruah of Bard College and his family, who hosted my stay in Guwahati. Professor Baruah also kindly gave me opportunities to present and publish my articles on the Nellie incident.

I was fortunate enough to interact with scholars who were very active in either supporting or opposing the antiforeigner movement. I would like to thank Professor Basant Deka, who shared his views on the movement as well as some important documents published at the time. Professor Amalendu

Guha and Professor Hiren Gohain also took the time to read some of my articles and give their comments, and it was a great privilege to receive their feedback.

Professor Masami Sekine of Keio University was my teacher in my undergraduate years, and initial years of graduate studies. I would not have chosen to proceed to higher studies if I had not met him. Dr Nariaki Nakazato, Professor Emeritus of the University of Tokyo, kindly gave me institutional affiliation when I was a postdoctoral fellow at the Japan Society for the Promotion of Science. I have learned a lot from his strict attitude and passion towards research. Had it not been for his advice that I publish my work in English, this book would not have taken its present form. Professor Chiharu Takenaka of Rikkyo University kindly provided comments on my first article on the Nellie incident (now Chapter 6 of this book) and has since been a tremendous source of support and encouragement.

Most of this book was written when I was working as a Research Associate at the International Peace Research Institute of Meiji Gakuin University. It was a great pleasure to interact with my senior colleagues there, and they always showed understanding of and interest in my work. I would like to express special thanks to Professor Makoto Katsumata, Director of the Institute, and Professor Shigeki Takeo, former Director, as well as the many staff members who supported my work.

The research in this book would not have been possible without my interviews with survivors and attackers in the Nellie incident. I would like to thank both these groups of people for sharing their painful experiences with me, a foreigner. This book is dedicated to them. I am grateful to Mrs Rina Pator, who hosted my stay in Nellie, and her brother Mr Pranab Pator, who accompanied me on most of my interviews in the Nellie area. Also, Dr Rejaul Karim accompanied me to Nellie in 2007 and helped me interact with Muslims in the area. I gained a deeper understanding of Muslim society in Assam through him.

I am most grateful to the family of late Pranab Baruah, an eminent Assamese painter, for permitting me to use his painting "Immortal Bliss" on the cover of this book. During my fieldwork in the Nellie area, I had a chance to visit his home at Nagaon and saw the painting. It left me with a deep impression and I'd been wishing to use the painting whenever my work was finalized and I had a chance to publish it.

Three years of study at Jawaharlal Nehru University brought me lots of joy as well as hardship. With the help of friends, especially fellow Japanese students studying at the university, I was able to enjoy life on campus. In Assam, Xonzoi Borbora has always been a great friend, and he was the person who advised me to visit Nellie. Without his advice, this work would have never taken place. Since then, Xonzoi has always given me advice and comments on my fieldwork and research, and also allowed me to use his office. My sincere thanks goes to Dolly, Sarat Phukan, Kazu, Bathari, Kunj and Anjuman, who kept me company during my lonely stay in Assam. I would also like to thank Malaya Ileto, who edited most of the first draft of this book, giving comments and encouraging me in the process. It was a great help as I made my lone effort to finalize the manuscript.

I would like to thank the Heiwa Nakajima Foundation (2001–2002) and Jawaharlal Nehru Memorial Fund (2003–2004) for granting scholarships for my PhD research. I was a postdoctoral fellow of the Japan Society for the Promotion of Science from 2004 to 2007, and this gave me enough time to reshape my doctoral thesis into a study on the Nellie incident. From 2008 to 2011, I was awarded a Grant-in-Aid for Young Scientists (B) by the Japan Society for the Promotion of Science, through which I made several research trips in finalizing this manuscript.

It would have been impossible to continue my studies without the help of my family. I would like to thank my parents and my sister, Saori, for always encouraging me and supporting my work. Last but not the least, I thank my partner, Yoshikazu Shiobara, who has always understood my work the most and been a source of great encouragement. He accompanied me on my first fieldwork trip to the Nellie area, and when I face difficulty, is always around to discuss things and offer help. This work owes more to him than anyone.

1

Introduction

On February 18, 1983, Nellie, a rural area in central Assam, witnessed an incident of large-scale violence and killing. It was in the immediate aftermath of the state's legislative assembly election. Nearly two thousand Muslim peasants of East Bengal origin were killed in the incident, which was an attack perpetrated by the residents of the area, which included the Assamese and the Tiwas, an indigenous[1] group inhabiting certain tracts of the plains of Assam. Known as the "Nellie Massacre," this infamous incident was reported widely all over India as a "tribal massacre" that took place in Assam. It was also reported as one of the biggest collective acts of violence in postcolonial India. The *Times of India* reported of the Nellie incident that after the Great Calcutta Killing in 1946, "Nothing so gruesome has disgraced India ever since the post-partition riots" (*Times of India*, February 22, 1983).

The incident attracted a great deal of attention at the time, but it was not sustained, and what happened in Nellie was not studied much afterwards. This, incidentally, is not an isolated case of selective amnesia. It is a phenomenon common to many acts of large-scale collective violence or so-called riots and is a major hurdle for researchers intending to undertake a serious study of the incident. The attackers were reluctant to give interviews and officials were unwilling to disclose information on the police investigation. Also, as will be discussed in the next section, violence was not a topic that was widely favored by sociologists or historians in general till the mid-1990s.

In the last decade, however, India has seen a tremendous increase in studies on collective violence. Whether it is in the discipline of history, sociology, anthropology, or political science, collective violence is one of the most discussed topics in the field of social sciences. The increase in the number of acts of communal violence, together with the rise of right-wing Hindu politics, has led scholars to examine the causes and circumstances leading to large-scale violence involving the masses.

Although there has been substantial progress in the study of collective violence, the so-called communal riots are still labeled as spontaneous acts conducted by uncontrolled mobs. Mass media, including print and electronic media, perceive communal violence as situated in places that lack "civilization." Newspapers reporting the Gujarat communal violence in 2002 used descriptions such as "the wounds of civilization" (*Frontline*, March 16, 2002) and commented, "When the rest of the world is moving ahead, we are sliding back to the medieval times" (*Times of India*, March 1, 2002).

While agreeing that the incidents of violence in Gujarat or Ayodhya were undoubtedly brutal and merit the most severe of criticisms, recent studies influenced by postmodern and postcolonial discourses have also extensively criticized such simplistic construction of "the civilized" and "the savage" dichotomy. Riot as "violence by uncontrolled mobs" was a typical notion shared by colonial British officials, who used it as an excuse for the colonial occupation of India and to "civilize the barbarous natives." Despite severe critiques of such views and notions, discourses on communal violence are still characterized by the dichotomy of "the civilized" and "the savage," and riots are placed as a symbol of untamed India. The term "barbaric mob" is often found implicit even in academic discourse regarding this type of violence. Despite the problematic character of terms such as "communalism" and "riot," they are still prevalent in contemporary India.

In recent years, there have been attempts by political scientists such as Paul Brass to analyze communal violence from an instrumentalist perspective. Brass focused on how politicians or leaders of large-scale organizations manipulate processes of collective violence and emphasized the aspect of riot production. However, by emphasizing the role of the elite too much, the participants of riots are made to appear as mere tools. There is no arguing that the issue of manipulation by the elite is important in the study of riots. However, by focusing only on the leaders, there has been a tendency to disregard the masses merely as objects to be mobilized or utilized.

Such a model might be relevant in terms of particular cases of collective violence in contemporary South Asia. For instance, it explains how Hindu–Muslim "communal" violence became prominent since the late 1980s with the rise of the right-wing Hindu political parties. However, the so-called attackers or tribal rioters do not fit into an explanation of the main focus of this book: the Nellie incident. Although there was strong leadership from student leaders in the antiforeigner movement, they were mainly based in the urban areas and did not have direct control in the rural areas. At the same time, the villagers who participated in the attack were more or less ordinary farmers and peasants, unlike the collective violence in urban India where the violence is triggered by *goonda*s or "criminal elements."

Then, is the Nellie incident an exceptional case? A closer examination of the Nellie incident would reveal that it also shares some common features with other episodes of collective violence in contemporary South Asia. We shall now examine some salient features of the incident in comparison with other incidents of collective violence in South Asia and explain what one can learn from the analysis of the Nellie incident.

Why Do Ordinary People Participate in Riots?: Agency of Rioters

There are several salient features of the collective violence, or so-called communal riots, which increased in numbers from the late 1980s: (1) Almost all the violence took place amongst the urban poor (Spencer 2003: 1569). (2) The violence happened in relation to movements by large-scale organizations (most notably religious organizations) and/or political parties. (3) The government was sympathetic to, or collaborated with the party concerned, and did not work effectively to prevent the violence by using law-enforcement actors (police and security forces). As a result, the culprits or attackers of violence were rarely punished, leading to the issue of impunity. It was especially salient in the cases of the Gujarat riot in 2002 and the Delhi riot in 1984. (4) There is a routinization of violence in specific towns and states (Brass 2003: 30, 37–39; Varshney 2002: 103).

The Nellie incident shares some of the features outlined but has substantial differences: (1) The incident took the form of the poor attacking each other, but in rural areas. (2) There was an influence of the student organization but it did not have direct control of the participants of the riot. (3) The local police did not take action promptly, but not because of any government order. The Congress[2] government simply did not have control over them. (4) There was no routinization of the violence, at least in the area. The survivors went back to their villages and lived side by side with the attackers for three decades.

The most notable difference is the role of the state government regarding the incident. In this incident, the Congress government had a will to protect the victims but they failed, partly because the violence triggered by the student organization's boycott was so widespread, and partly because the local police was sympathetic to the movement and did not take action. In other words, the law enforcement authorities got paralyzed in the clash between the government and the powerful movement leaders, and there was a vacuum of authority in the state. It was in this milieu that the local people decided to attack their neighbors. This is an incident where the agency of the rioters is visible and salient, when compared to other events of large-scale collective violence in India.

The primary aim of this book is to analyze why common people participate in riots and how they live with memories of violence after the event. The villagers who participated in the attack in the Nellie area are ordinary peasants who struggle for their daily survival. It is difficult to find any substantial difference between the villagers from Nellie and those from other villages in rural Assam. However, they participated in the attack and massacred 2,000 neighbors in one day. Crucially, they continue to live in the locality along with the survivors.

An analysis of the incident will allow one to understand how and why ordinary people participate in violence. Although the Nellie incident stands out as a prominent case in which ordinary people participated, it is incorrect to recognize it as an exceptional case. It might be true that incidents are triggered by political leaders who use professional thugs and troublemakers, but there are also cases where ordinary people get embroiled in riots while the incident expands. In some cases, urban middle-class people participated in the riots. It was especially true in the case of the anti-Sikh riots in Delhi in 1984 and the anti-Tamil riots in Colombo in 1983 (Tambiah 1996: 280, 282–87).

Thus, labeling rioters as *goonda*s or "criminal elements" and treating them as "Others" would entail overlooking some aspects crucial to the analysis of collective violence in India today, as riots are not always characterized by the ubiquity of the *goonda* or criminal elements manipulated by politicians participating in the process.

It is true, nonetheless, that the analysis of the agency of the participants of riots is a sensitive and difficult task. In emphasizing their autonomous perspectives and actions, there is the possibility of such analyses averting attention from the involvement and responsibility of political parties or large-scale ethnic/religious organizations. Therefore, it is essential to also focus on the role of large-scale organizations and political parties to understand the politics and power relations in the area, while analyzing the agency of rioters.

Regarding the Nellie incident, the majority of the participants were rural peasants belonging to indigenous communities or from the lower strata of the caste system, categorized as Scheduled Castes or Other Backward Classes. Being the first inhabitants of the Brahmaputra valley, the indigenous communities had an unquestioned legitimacy within Assam. The victims were also peasants, but were migrants from East Bengal, now independent Bangladesh. Both groups are minorities in Assam, and their voices are underrepresented in reportage and other writings on, or accounts of, the incident. This book is also an attempt to analyze the agency of subalterns by recording these voices and examining how they perceived the event. In order to focus on their perspectives, the analysis will be drawn mainly from the narratives of the victims and attackers in the Nellie incident.

In this analysis, the assumption is that the participants of the violence made rational decisions and joined the attack. Therefore, it is not the intention of this book to analyze their actions from the perspective of crowd psychology. The aim is to analyze the decision-making process by examining their narratives to overcome the stereotypical assumption that the rioters were "barbaric tribes" or members of an "uncontrollable mob."

Collective Violence and Ethnic/Social Movements

Many acts of collective violence do not occur unexpectedly, however spontaneous they seem to. They can be the consequences of processes and events such as xenophobic movements and their ideologies, the mobilization of masses, political crises such as election trouble or the demise of a political leader, or the instigation and support of political parties or large-scale religious groups. These reasons have played an important role in many instances of large-scale collective violence, such as the violence during the partition of India and the anti-Sikh riots in Delhi in 1984. The Nellie incident also saw reasons among these. The antiforeigner movement that began in Assam in 1979 provided the ideological backdrop to the mobilization of the masses. During the continuum of this movement that rode a wave of mass support, the imposition of elections by the Congress-led government in Assam resulted in large-scale dissent and disturbance not only in Nellie, but all over the state. This disturbance, and various other reasons that will be discussed later, contributed to many incidents of violence in that period, Nellie being the largest in scale.

Although collective violence often occurs in relation to large-scale movements led by ethnic, social, or political organizations, it is often taken as an aberration and excluded from the mainstream analyses of movements. The strategy of the leaders or the so-called elite is the focus in most analyses of ethnic or social movements. The major objects of analyses tend to be organizational structures, ideologies, strategies, and negotiations with power-holders by the leaders. This has been particularly prominent in rational choice theory and resource mobilization theory.

If we revert to the early phases of the study of social movements, we will find that the collective behavior approach emerged from studies of "crowd psychology." This approach analyzed social movements together with mass panic, craze, hostile outbursts, and riots. For a long time, these events were regarded as demonstrating the breakdown of the social order and social disintegration, meaning something abnormal and unusual.

Things changed a little in the 1960s and 1970s. As a reaction to the emergence of the civil rights, anti-war, women's, and black movements, the focus shifted to resource mobilization theory, which sought to rehabilitate social movements by reincorporating them into the realm of rational action and organizational politics. Social movements came to be analyzed as rational undertakings by movement entrepreneurs who accomplish the constitution of a collective project by their mobilizing efforts (Fuchs and Linkenbach 2003: 1526–31).

Later on, when new social movements became the focus of the studies, movements began to be recognized as a normal feature of society, and regarded as more institutionalized rather than exceptional or deviant. Social movements became one of the major areas of studies in sociology (Fuchs and Linkenbach 2003: 1526–31). It is noteworthy, however, that situating social movements in the mainstream of social sciences has created a disjuncture between social movements and collective violence or riots, thus marginalizing the latter's analysis.

The Nellie incident has been situated, thus far, within the discourse of uncontrolled violence carried out by tribal people where the leaders of the Assam movement have denied responsibility. This book will look at the relationship between two political epochs of Assam—the movement led by the middle-class student leaders and the incident led by the Assamese and the Tiwa peasants of the rural areas. It will attempt to analyze the Nellie incident as one of the central events during the antiforeigner movement in Assam. The incident was not directly controlled by the top student leaders, but it was an important outcome of the movement.

Chapter 5, in particular, will focus on the decision-making process of the attackers and analyze their agency in the incident. The argument thus far has been that they were merely utilized by the leaders (of the movement). However, a close examination of the situation at the time reveals that there was a certain decision-making process among the village elders of the Tiwas before the attack. There was a pall of fear at the time of an attack on the Assamese and the Tiwa people of the area by a fresh group of "foreigners," a fear generated by rumors that outsiders had come from another village and attacked Bihari peasants nearby. The perpetrators of this attack were allegedly hidden in the Muslim villages. Belief in the rumors prompted the Assamese and Tiwa peasants of the area to decide on an attack on these Muslim villages in the manner of what is called a preemptive strike.

The examination of the relationship between the attackers' role and the leadership of the student organization is the most interesting exercise in the analysis of this incident. Leaders of the antiforeigner movement, mainly students and the urban middle class, provided the ideology and legitimacy for ostracizing "foreigners" in Assam. As for the local residents near Nellie—the Tiwas and the Assamese peasants—they suffered from land grabbing by the Muslims. In rural Assam, many people mortgage their land but, unable to pay, have it taken away, and they are subsequently forced to migrate or work as daily-wage laborers or *adhiyar*s (sharecroppers). Such situation is prevalent in Nagaon[3] district, where the colonization scheme was introduced and large-scale immigration took place. In the northern part of the district, the Muslims were already a majority and the indigenous peoples had slowly lost their land. In the Nellie area, the pressure on land was becoming more acute. Under such circumstances, the Tiwas and the Other Backward Classes supported the movement, and the movement leaders and local residents fought a joint struggle.

However, it was not that the two groups' interests or interpretation of the aim of the movement met completely with each other's: it was not only regarding their stake in the movement that they differed, but also in their perception of the movement's target. By their slogans and other forms of expression, the leaders of the movement advocated the deportation of "foreigners." However, the victims of this particular violent incident were mainly the Muslim peasants of Bengali origin who had immigrated during the colonial period. On the one hand, it can be deduced that the urban middle-class elite's concepts of "foreigner" and "citizenship" were interpreted in a different way in the rural areas. But, on the other hand, the attackers were also aware of and acknowledged the difference between the Muslim peasants who had settled in the area long before the more recent lot came into the region and those who were described as foreigners. It can thus be analyzed that the Assamese and the Tiwa populace utilized the movement and the election disturbance in order to get rid of the Muslim peasants who were slowly grabbing their land and eating into their resources.

Apart from these points, I would also like to focus on the memory of this violent incident and its impact on the construction of identity among the Muslim peasants and the Tiwas. It is, however, worth the effort to highlight the background of the antiforeigner movement before discussing this point.

The Antiforeigner Movement in Assam: 1979–1985

The six years from 1979 to 1985 saw a heightened prominence of the issue of foreign nationals in Assamese society (mostly East Pakistani and Bangladeshi), and a large-scale movement emerged against the inclusion of foreigners in the electoral rolls. The movement was led by the All Assam Students' Union (AASU), which managed to garner significant public support. The influence of the AASU and the movement can be read from the fact that they were able to call for a general boycott of the assembly elections in 1983.

It is widely known that the movement emerged against the backdrop of continued immigration to Assam from the East Bengal region since the colonial period. What triggered the movement into its increased relevance was an abnormal increase in the number of voters on the electoral roll. Based on this, the AASU was successful in organizing a large-scale popular movement. The leaders of the antiforeigner movement demanded the deletion of the names of foreigners from the voters' list, based on the rights of citizenship and consonant with the clauses in the Indian Constitution. While the movement itself took a peaceful path, numerous violent incidents of ethnic and religious nature dotted its course, notably during the state assembly election in 1983.

It was in 1978 that the issue of foreign nationals started to attract the attention of the people of Assam for the first time. It began with the need for a by-election caused by the death of Member of Parliament Hiralal Patwari and this Lok Sabha by-election was for the Mangaldoi parliamentary constituency. In the course of the electoral process, it was discovered that the number of voters in the constituency had gone up phenomenally. This prompted the AASU to demand a deferral of the election and the deletion of the names of foreign nationals from the electoral rolls. This marked the beginning of six years of agitation in Assam, popularly known as the antiforeigner movement.

The movement gained mass support, and became very active by late 1979. Early 1980 saw several rounds of talks on the question of deportation of illegal immigrants between the AASU leaders and the then Prime Minister, Indira Gandhi. While the leaders of the movement demanded that all those who entered Assam after 1951 be deported, the government proposed 1971 as the cutoff date.[4] This conflict in demands and guidelines resulted in the talks being inconclusive.

The progression of the movement also shifted political course. In the latter part of 1980, the central government became oppressive towards the movement. Mass support also waned with time and all these factors led to the stagnation of the movement from 1981 to 1982. Late 1982 saw the movement rising to its feet again with the decision of the central government to hold an election in Assam without revising the electoral rolls. The organizers of the movement called for a boycott of the election, and a number of violent incidents occurred during this period—the Nellie massacre being one of the biggest. It is estimated that more than 1,600 people died in the daylong attack.

The violence managed to draw lines between ethnic and communal identities. Also, the trajectory that the movement took highlighted many questions. The movement actually had started out for protection of the rights of the Assamese people, which were perceived as threatened because of Bengali middle-class dominance in various sectors and an increase in the population of "foreigners." How this nonviolent movement to safeguard rights translated itself into a communal riot against the Muslim immigrants of East Bengal origin could be considered a crucial point in the analysis of the incident.

The background to the antiforeigner movement and the violence thereof lies with the construction of nation-states: one with the partition of India and the communal violence that accompanied it, and the other with the independence of Bangladesh in 1971. Although the general perception puts Hindu–Muslim communal tension as low in Assam compared with other regions, the propaganda of the "threat of the Muslims" also exists. There is a tendency to regard almost all the Muslims as "Bangladeshis," despite the fact that a large number of these Muslims are descendants of immigrants from East Bengal during the colonial period.

The antiforeigner movement in Assam shares the character of the so-called nativist movements or movements by "sons of the soil" that can be seen in other states in India, and some decolonized states in Asia and Africa. These tend to be reactionary and opp ssive towards minorities such as the Muslims or immigrants in the region. Such types of movements are often seen in states where the majority's power basis is fragile due to a colonial system that still prevails in various forms even after the beginning of the process of decolonization. In the case of Assam, one can see that employment in the modern sectors that came with colonization was dominated by immigrants brought by the colonizers. Moreover, the two main industries in the state—tea and oil—are not controlled by the Assamese. While foreign or Indian companies outside the state own and control the former from London or Calcutta, the central government controls the latter.

Movements emerge when a change in the power structure is brought about by the process of decolonization to the postcolonial polity, and when the "sons of the soil" enter middle-class occupations. The process of a struggle to consolidate power in a country or state leads to the oppression of minorities. Such phenomenon is not unique to Assam but is common to other postcolonial countries such as Malaysia or Fiji, where the original inhabitants were socially and economically subordinate under the colonial system.

Right after the independence of India, the "sons of the soil" movement in Assam targeted the middle-class Bengalis (mostly Hindus) who occupied a large number of administrative posts under the British colonial system and other occupations in the modern sector. The establishment of Calcutta as the first capital of the colonizers facilitated the middle-class Bengalis towards access to higher education and, consequently, administrative jobs under the colonial system. The colonial expansion to Assam brought this Bengali population of colonial officials there, and in due course, they managed to attain a strong social and economic position in the region. The conflict took place when the emerging Assamese middle class, mostly a caste-Hindu population, tried to introduce Assamese as the official language of the state of Assam and as the medium of instruction at Gauhati University. The middle-class Bengalis were the most vocal opponents of this policy, along with a section of indigenous tribal peoples in Assam. This conflict led to several protests and demonstrations in the Bengali-dominated areas.

Thus, the antiforeigner movement was also obliquely regarded as another attempt to drive out middle-class Bengalis, mostly Hindus, from the state. Fierce opposition came from West Bengal, along with middle-class Bengalis in Assam, notably Cachar District where Bengali-speaking populations are dominant. Questions were raised over the legitimacy of the claims of the movement, and the Bengali media was mostly against the movement. Not surprisingly, the beginning of the movement saw a confrontation between the Assamese middle class and the Bengali middle class.

However, when violence broke out in the rural areas of Assam, it was turned against the Muslim peasants of East Bengal origin. This was partly due to political change in the state. Until the late 1970s, the Congress was the dominant party in Assam. However, after the split of the party in 1977, the Janata party became the ruling party in Assam for the first time since independence. The decline of Congress' influence gave an opportunity to emerging regional parties to expand their strength. It should be noted that from the beginning of the movement, two small-scale political parties, Purbanchaliya Lok Parishad and Assam Jatiyatabadi Dal, joined the antiforeigner agitation. Thus, it was clear from the beginning of the movement that the leaders sought to establish a regional political platform independent of the Congress and other pan-Indian political parties. In fact, the student leaders formed a political party called Asom Gana Parishad (AGP) in early 1985, after the movement came to an end.

Till the mid-1970s, both the Assamese Hindus and the Muslims of immigrant origin were a strong support base for the Congress party. However, when the antiforeigner movement started, although the Muslims of East Bengal origin supported the movement in its initial phase, realizing that they had also became the target of attack, they turned their back on the student leaders and expected the Congress party to provide them with shelter. On the other hand, the middle-class, caste-Hindu Assamese and a section of the indigenous population supported the movement enthusiastically. In this way, with the emergence of the AASU and the subsequent formation of the AGP, the traditional vote banks of the Congress split into two. For the newly emerged middle-class leadership, in order to undermine the solid Congress support base, the Muslims of immigrant origin were easy target.

Thus, the antiforeigner movement can also be seen as a prominent case of the rise of regionalism and large-scale political change that prevailed not only in Assam but also in other parts of India. Demands for regionalism, which were active in Punjab and Assam in the early 1980s, invited a harsh response from the Government of India (GOI) led by Indira Gandhi. It should be noted that two large-scale incidents of collective violence—the Nellie massacre in 1983 and the anti-Sikh riots in Delhi in 1984—were related to regional nationalism in these areas, and partly invited by reactions to oppression by the GOI.

During the movement, and especially during the state legislative assembly election in 1983, the confrontation among the different ethnic groups, notably the local Assamese and the Muslims of immigrant origin, were articulated. In this circumstance, the AASU and the other movement leaders enjoyed mass support from most of the sections of Assam, but such strong and overwhelming support did not last long. For example, the plains indigenous tribes of Assam, who suffered from land alienation, supported the movement when that particular issue was raised by the movement leaders. When the movement did little to solve their problems, the movement leaders slowly lost their support among these people. Their dissatisfaction led them to believe that the movement leaders had just used the issue in order to mobilize them in the movement. Movements for autonomy became prominent among the plains tribes of Assam, including the Tiwas, after this chapter of the antiforeigner movement.

The antiforeigner movement, thus, wittingly or unwittingly, started many political processes in Assam. It can be related to the triggering of movements for autonomy among many ethnic groups of Assam, and also marking the beginning of the Muslim peasants being perceived in Assam as the important "Other." An analysis of the Nellie incident leads invariably to the question of ethnic divide in Assam, where a greater Assamese nationality that included all the ethnic groups was once imagined.

The antiforeigner movement was the most successful among the series of Assamese nationality movements. Ironically, however, the struggle over nationality led to the various minority, autochthonous, ethnic groups becoming increasingly aware of their marginalized status. At the same time, it positioned the Muslims of East Bengal origin as the "Other." All these points led to a divide in the Assamese nationality question. In this regard, the Nellie incident was a significant symbolic event that marked the beginning of the movements for autonomy and rights by the indigenous groups, as well as the construction of the category of "Other" for the Muslims of East Bengal origin.

Memory and Violence

How do the rioters and victims remember collective violence and narrate it, and live with the memory of violence? How are these memories related to identity when the ethnic issue is involved? During fieldwork in the Nellie area where the violence took place, I noticed that the Tiwa narratives on the incident were often connected to the autonomous movement that was (and is still) active among them. This movement, presently led by the All Tiwa Students' Union (ATSU), began in the late 1980s, and hence, was not directly related to the Nellie incident, but the two are closely intertwined in the psyche of the Tiwa people, particularly those deeply involved in the movement for autonomy.

To study this relationship, we need to turn our attention to discussions on collective memory. Halbwachs (1950) argued that the past is a social construction, mainly, if not wholly, shaped by the concerns of the present. This is called the "presentist approach," and Halbwachs was the first soci- ologist to stress this point. In other words, the mental images we employ to solve present problems influence our conceptions of the past. So, collective memory is essentially a reconstruction of the past. Although a too-pronounced presentism is modified by works of later scholars, Halbwachs' approach remains the basic premise in analyzing memory.

In Chapter 6 of this book, I focus on the relationship between collective identities of minority groups and memories of violence. Compared to the established nations that have already developed an official national history, minority groups in nation-states (so-called ethnic, religious or linguistic minorities, or tribes) have to choose a strategy regarding whether or not to articulate their collective identities. More recently, we can see tendencies of minority groups becoming politically aware and organizing movements. There are still, however, groups that do not (or cannot) choose to claim their rights as a specific group and assimilate with dominant nations.

When a minority group chooses to distinguish itself from the dominant nation and attempts to establish its own identity, members of the group need to narrate their own history and define themselves as subjects in and of it. If the group chooses to assimilate, it does not need its own version of history. In the Nellie massacre, the group generally recognized as the attackers is active in developing its own version of narratives on the violence, whereas the victim group is not.

In this massacre, the interrelation of the groups is very complicated, since both the attackers and the victims of the massacre were economically, politically, and socially subordinate groups of Assamese society. Here, we can see a problem in the way the minorities establish their own version of the narrative against the master narrative, and the way they distance themselves from the dominant group.

The master narrative on the Nellie incident in Assam is largely shared by the middle-class Assamese. For them, the incident is a stain in their otherwise successful mass-mobilized movement. The rioters and the victims, however, remember the violence in a different way.

Narratives on the memory of violence are not mediated by newspapers and other written media in the rural areas. Unlike the memories of the urban middle class, they do not have a pattern of narratives that is found elsewhere. These vary widely in different areas and villages. In the case of the Tiwa villagers who participated in the riot, they largely share the feelings of anger and betrayal against the movement leaders and the Assamese as a whole. In their view, the Tiwas helped the Assamese, only to be accused by the movement leaders of taking the events out of control when violence broke out. Their deep resentment lies in the fact that the movement leaders escaped without sharing responsibility for the incident, leaving them to be considered as the sole perpetrators.

The narrative of the Tiwas seems to be deeply related to the fact that they started a movement for their rights and autonomy. While the feeling of betrayal is largely shared across all Tiwa areas and villages, the tendency for a disjunction with the mainstream Assamese is more prevalent in villages where the ATSU, one of the central organizations of the movement, is active. Being an indigenous minority, the Tiwa movement has legitimacy within Assam, and hence does not fear consequences of oppression or pressure for assimilation from the mainstream community.

On the other hand, the Muslims are not very vocal in narrating their memories of the incident. In many villages, they were reluctant to talk about it. Instead of a coherent thread in their narratives, there were fragmented ones, such as that "the incident was a retaliation for their casting vote in the election despite AASU's boycott." Because of the fear of deportation and lack of legitimacy in land ownership, there is no strong process of identity formation or the emergence of a movement among the Muslim peasants in the area. The only articulated voice from this community is seen in the memoranda for compensation and rehabilitation submitted to the GOI in 1983, 1991, and 2007.

This does not mean that the Muslims are not interested in bringing justice to the attackers or improving their marginalized status. However, cornered in a small pocket in mixed areas, they do not have the social space to articulate their demands or grievances. Being targeted as "foreigners" by the AGP and the AASU, the only force they can rely on is the Congress party. What is interesting is that their minority status is one of the reasons that the Muslim peasants were not vocal about the incident and were reluctant to differentiate themselves from the Assamese.

Organization of the Book

As is clear from what has been discussed thus far, this book's subject is the relationship between the agency of riot participants, and the issues of memory of violence and the collective identity of the attackers and survivors in the Nellie incident.

Chapter 2 deals with the theoretical background for collective violence in contemporary South Asia. As has been discussed, after the two large-scale incidents of violence in Colombo (1983) and Delhi (1984), and the rise of the so-called Hindu–Muslim communal riot in relation to the emergence of Hindu right-wing political parties, there has been a growing concern among social scientists about collective violence in this region. A close look at some of the major works on the issue reveals that there are a number of studies from the 1980s and the 1990s on survivors of violence and the relationship between collective violence and politics. However, it becomes clear that a study on the actual participants in the riots is very rare due to the difficulty of collecting any kind of survey material.

In that chapter, I attempt to search for a methodology for studying riot participants, especially in the case of rural riots, such as the Nellie incident, through interviews with both the attackers and the survivors of the incident. The Nellie incident has a specific character in that it saw little intervention or manipulation by political parties or large-scale organizations. By examining their role in the event, the need to analyze the issue of agency of the rioters arises in this case. At the same time, in the last part of the chapter, I touch upon the issue of memory of violence. The narratives of the attackers and survivors are deeply connected to their identity formation, and examining how the collective memory on violence revolves around the identity of the group is key in understanding how their narratives sometimes differ from what are considered facts.

Chapter 3 attempts to locate the antiforeigner movement in the historical context of the nationalist movement and the formation of nationality in Assam. It also analyzes the character of the movement in comparison with earlier movements on the linguistic issue. During the colonial period, there were three occasions when Assamese nationalist aspirations became prominent. The first was at the time of the colonization of Assam by the British and the Bengali language was introduced as the medium for colonial administration. The second occasion was in the early 1900s as a reaction to the introduction of immigration policy from the Bengal region. At the same time, controversy over the Line System, which tried to control the settlement of immigrants, attracted society's wide attention. The third occasion was at the time of partition, when the Assam Pradesh Congress Committee opposed the plan to transfer Assam to Pakistan.

In the postcolonial period, the issue of language reemerged during the debate over the official language of the state. In this movement, middle-class Bengalis, mostly Hindus, became a major target. Thus, the advent of the movement in 1979 encountered fierce opposition from middle-class Bengalis in West Bengal and Assam, particularly from the Barak Valley[5] areas such as Cachar. Their first interpretation of the movement was that it was another attempt to drive out outsiders, primarily Bengalis. However, the antiforeigner movement had some salient features that were different from the linguistic movement in the 1960s and the 1970s. In the former movement, mass mobilization was successful because the movement leaders tried to bring attention to land issues that affected people in the rural areas, especially indigenous groups in plain areas. By focusing on the issue of acute shortage of land, the target of movement was shifted from middle-class, largely Hindu Bengalis, to the Muslim peasants of immigrant origin.

Chapter 4 focuses on the relationship between the movement leaders and the participants in the attack in the Nellie incident. After describing the political circumstances that led to the violent reaction during the state legislative assembly election and giving a chronological account of the event, the chapter attempts to look at how the movement and its leaders were relevant to, but not directly manipulating, the massacre. It also tries to establish a model for analyzing rural collective violence, particularly that in the Nellie incident, which is different from that of the peasant insurgency in the colonial period and, also, of Hindu–Muslim communal riots in contemporary India.

The latter part of the chapter analyzes both official and non-official inquiry commissions on the disturbance during the election. A critical analysis of the commission reports reveals that both commissions were used to legitimize either the GOI or the movement leaders, and put blame on each other.

Chapter 5 focuses on the narratives of the attackers in the Nellie incident, particularly regarding their decision making. In one of the interviews, a local student leader from the village at the time referred to smaller incidents in which Tiwa villagers were attacked by the Muslims. There was also a rumor that the Muslim outsiders would come to nearby villages and harass the Assamese and Tiwa villagers. According to his account, the Tiwas and other Assamese villagers felt their safety threatened, and this led the villagers to decide to attack the Muslims in the neighboring villages.

This account shows that self-defense, rather than land issues or movement ideology, played an important role in decision making among the villagers. This does not mean that the ideology of the antiforeigner movement or land alienation were irrelevant to the movement; they were important factors in demarcating the boundary between who the attackers and victims were. My argument is that it is misleading to state that the villagers were controlled by the movement leaders or communal forces. The riot participants reinterpreted the land issues or the antiforeigner movement in their own perspective, based on their everyday interaction with the Muslim peasants of immigrant origin.

Chapter 6 deals with the narratives of the Tiwas and the Muslim peasants in the Nellie incident. The Tiwas started their own movement for autonomy immediately after the AASU movement and tried to differentiate themselves from the Assamese. On the other hand, the Muslims have had no other option but to remain and assimilate with Assamese nationality. This difference in strategy emerges from the narratives on the incident. The grievance against the "betrayal" of the Assamese leadership is most prominent among the Tiwas, as the following narrative shows: "Although we supported the Assamese in the movement and helped them in the attack, they did not take responsibility and escaped. They put the blame solely on the Tiwas." On the other hand, there are fragmented narratives among the Muslims that mourn the violence; yet they are unable to create an alternative identity.

Both the Tiwas and the Muslims are subordinate communities in Assam. However, (for various reasons such as their indigenous status) the Tiwas are more successful in obtaining their social and political spaces and creating a counter-discourse against the Assamese mainstream through their autonomous movement. On the other hand, the Muslims are numerically strong and economically successful in the Nellie area, but they do not have their own media or organizations that justly represent their issues and causes. Thus, this chapter explores the relationship between identity formation and the narratives of a historical event, and attempts to analyze how differences prominently appear in narratives of violence.

The concluding chapter begins with an account of my revisit to Nellie area in August 2007. Contrary to my earlier research, this time, the survivors in the village were vocal in narrating their pain and accusations of the movement leaders at the time. The fact that the Congress was in power in the state for more than seven years gave them assurance that they will not be targeted even if they demand compensation in the Nellie area.

Since the end of the antiforeigner movement, there have emerged other types of nationalist movements in Assam. The Bodo movement, which was one of the most active movements in Assam in the 1990s and 2000s, has led to violent clashes or, more precisely, ethnic killings where outsiders have become the easy target of frustrated ethnic groups (often armed). There are similar clashes among other ethnic communities in Assam and there is no prospect that the situation will improve in the near future. The people in Assam and many other parts of South Asia are subject to "riots." In other words, anyone can become victim to collective violence. More importantly, it is possible for anyone to become an attacker in collective violence.

In the Nellie area, both the immigration issue and land alienation, which provided the background for the attack, were solved. At the same time, the compensation and remedies for the survivors remain unresolved. In such a situation, rather than official, judicial prosecution or compensation, there is an urgent need for a community-based reconciliation process. The chapter concludes with the suggestion that although a political process is crucial in improving the present situation in Assam, an initiative for a community-based solution between the survivors and the attackers of the Nellie incident will be able to throw light on the long-standing ethnic killings in the area and in Assam.

Notes

1. The term "tribe" was introduced to India by British colonial officials and has a strong discriminatory connotation on the autochthonous ethnic communities in Northeast India and other parts of the country. With the rise of the indigenous movement in the international arena, there is an attempt to replace it with terms such as "indigenous peoples," a welcome move. Following from this, I would like to use the term "indigenous" in this book when referring to autochthonous ethnic communities. However, in the context of the Nellie incident, it is sometimes confusing to use the term "indigenous" because other Assamese-speaking communities, such as the caste-Hindu Assamese and the Hiras, are also regarded as "natives" when compared to the descendants of Muslim immigrants of Bengal origin. Hence, although I acknowledge the problem, I will sometimes use terms such as "indigenous tribal group" in order to make a clear distinction between autochthonous ethnic groups and other communities.

2. Unless otherwise noted, "Congress" stands for the Indian National Congress (before 1969) and the Congress (I).

3. Nagaon District was spelt in anglicized form, "Nowgong," till the mid-1980s. In this book, I use "Nagaon" which is closer to the Assamese pronunciation.

4. The AASU demanded 1951 as the cutoff year because the National Register of the Citizens was taken that year. The government, on the other hand, offered 1971 since that was when Bangladesh became independent from Pakistan.

5. The Barak Valley is situated in the southern part of Assam and adjacent to Sylhet District in Bangladesh. Due to its geographical condition, the majority of the population are Bengali-speaking, who settled in the area in the colonial period, particularly during the partition of India and Pakistan. The Assamese-dominant area of the northern part of the state is called the Brahmaputra valley.

2

How to Interpret "Riots": Theories on Collective Violence and the Question of Agency in Contemporary South Asia

Since the mid-1980s, studies on collective violence in South Asia have developed both in quality and quantity. With the emergence of so-called communal riots such as large-scale violence in urban areas in India and Sri Lanka, and the rise of right-wing Hindu organizations and disturbances most typically represented by the Ayodhya incident, social scientists in South Asia have started to tackle the issue of collective violence more than ever. In particular, the anti-Tamil riots that took place in Colombo, Sri Lanka, in 1983 and the anti-Sikh riots that took place in Delhi, India, in 1984 have had a tremendous impact on the scholars of these two countries. At the same time, together with the rise of the Bharatiya Janata Party (BJP), the right-wing Hindu political party, the so-called Hindu–Muslim communal riots have become a major political issue in the country. It has compelled scholars to reconsider the relationship between politics and violence in contemporary India.

On the other hand, 1997 marked the 50th anniversary of India's Independence, as well as of the large-scale violence that took place at the time of the Partition, between the Hindus, the Sikhs, and the Muslims. In the discipline of history, the study of collective violence, particularly Partition violence, has become a major concern for scholars. As a result, since the late 1980s, a large number of studies on collective violence has emerged in the disciplines of political science, history, sociology, and anthropology, and provided new perspectives in the understanding of "riots" and "mobs," which are traditionally recognized as "spontaneous" and "abnormal phenomena."

To point out some of the important arguments, at the outset, the relationship between colonialism and so-called communal violence was questioned.

Gyanendra Pandey, a leading historian of the Subaltern Studies Group, analyzed the colonial officers' descriptions of "communal violence." In such descriptions, "natives" were always positioned as the "primitive Other," and "native violence" was described using terms such as "religion," "fanaticism," and "ignorance," and recognized as a product of the absence of Enlightenment from Western education. Their presumption was that the Hindus and the Muslims were essentially violent communities and peoples, liable to break out into violence at any time unless "civilized" (Pandey 1994: 195–197). We should not overlook that such discourse constituted an important part of the West's "mission" to civilize the natives and thus contributed to the legitimacy of colonial domination.

At the same time, the need to review concepts such as "riots" and "communalism" has been called for. Even now, in the disciplines of political science and sociology, "riots" are seen as natural and collective outbursts, an aberration by the mobs without any rational aim. However, if we examine the phenomenon known as "riots" in contemporary South Asia, many do not fit into such a model. Thus, there is a need to rethink concepts such as "riots" and "mobs" in order to understand this type of violence in contemporary political and social contexts. As we can point out stereotypes and biases inherent in such concepts frequently used in the social sciences, scholars have begun recently to use the term "collective violence."

At the same time, it is difficult to completely replace the term "riot" with "collective violence," as the latter does not express some of the meaning of the former. For example, according to Horowitz, a riot is an intense, sudden, though not necessarily wholly unplanned, lethal attack by civilian members of one ethnic group on civilian members of another ethnic group, the victims chosen because of their group membership (Horowitz 2001: 1; Spencer 2003: 1564). In this book, as a theoretical concept, I would like to use the term "collective violence" as much as possible, but, as with many other scholars, the term "riot" will also be used interchangeably.

From the 1990s, there emerged a perspective of reconsidering the relationship between collective violence and politics, especially that of party politics. In contemporary India, it has been pointed out that most collective violence takes place at the time of elections. Notably, Paul Brass argued that collective violence is "produced" by political parties and large-scale organizations, stating that there is an "institutionalized riot system" in "riot-prone cities" (Brass 2003). This type of argument is important in overcoming the primordialist assumption that riots are caused by primordial ethnic or religious confrontations. At the same time, the emphasis on control by political parties has led to the image of participants in riots being "ignorant mobs" or *goondas* (criminals), and underestimates the issue of participation by "ordinary people" in collective violence or the agency of the masses during violence.

In this chapter, in order to analyze the Nellie incident, a case of large-scale collective violence, it is important to take note of the outcomes of studies about contemporary violence in South Asia. This incident shares many of the characteristics seen in other parts of India and Sri Lanka. For example, it took place during the religious/ethnic movement and in relation to the State Legislative Assembly election. That collective violence takes place in relation with mass-mobilized movements and party politics is often pointed out in studies on collective violence or so-called communal riots in India.

However, two things stand out in the Nellie incident, which make it quite different from other cases of such violence. One is that it took place in a rural area, while most other such incidents take place in urban areas. The other point is scale, with a death toll in Nellie of 2,000, making it one of the biggest riot incidents in contemporary South Asia, the others being the anti-Tamil riots in Colombo in 1983, the anti-Sikh riots in Delhi in 1984, the Bhagalpur riots in 1989, the Bombay riots in 1993 and the Gujarat violence in 2002. In my understanding, it was the only occasion of a large-scale riot in a rural part of India since the Partition violence. Thus, in addition to the major findings of studies on collective violence, this chapter will focus on examining studies on the agency of rioters and violence in rural India.

The 1983 Colombo Riots and the 1984 Delhi Riots: An Urge to Reconsider Collective Violence in South Asia

It was in the latter part of the 1980s that a number of arguments on collective violence emerged in the areas of sociology and social anthropology. Until then, there were some studies on "riots" or "communalism" in political science[1] and history, but there were few that focused on the subject in the disciplines of sociology and social anthropology.

However, the anti-Tamil riots in Colombo in 1983 and the anti-Sikh riots in Delhi in 1984, two large-scale incidents of collective violence that took place in the capital cities of Sri Lanka and India, attracted the attention of scholars in these countries, and they began to work on the issue in order to understand these phenomena, which were once thought to have been "overcome" through modernization. The two incidents claimed more than 3,000 lives, and led to a reconsideration of the assumption that large-scale riots would no longer occur in contemporary South Asia. Henceforth, the study of collective violence became a major issue in the discipline of social sciences in the region. Here, I introduce some of the major works on these incidents.

At the outset, Uma Chakravarti and Nandita Haksar published *Delhi Riots: Three Days in the Life of a Nation* (1987). Chakravarti was a historian at the University of Delhi. Nandita Haksar was her student, and later became a lawyer focusing on human right issues. They conducted intensive interviews with the survivors of the riot "to ensure that the experiences of the November carnage are recorded so that they are not altogether lost to the future historian," and thus, the main part of the book consists of transcribed scripts, which were tape-recorded during the interviews. In the preface, the authors stated that they felt "the need to present the experiences and perspectives of ordinary people as an alternative to the formal version of November riots," and hence chose not to publish an academic work but, rather, a compilation of interviews (Chakravarti and Haksar 1987: 9–11).

In 1990, Veena Das, then a scholar of sociology at the University of Delhi, edited a volume titled *Mirrors of Violence: Communities, Riots and Survivors in South Asia.* Based on seminar papers by historians, anthropologists, psychologists, and sociologists, the volume threw new light on the issue of collective violence in India and had a large-scale influence on studies in this area. Das, the editor, was involved in relief and rehabilitation work for survivors of the Delhi riot, particularly widows who had lost their husbands during the disturbance, and collected first-hand data on the issue. The last part of the volume consists of three papers on the narratives of the survivors of violence. Das emphasized the importance of narrating the experience of the survivors in her paper, stating, "[i]t is the special task of the survivors of violence to show us how such suffering may be transformed into redemption" (Das 1990: 33–34).

On the other hand, on the Colombo riot in Sri Lanka, Stanley Tambiah published *Leveling Crowds: Ethnonationalist Conflict and Collective Violence in South Asia* (1996). Tambiah is an anthropologist at Harvard University who experienced the violence while in Sri Lanka. Four case studies of collective violence in colonial and contemporary South Asia (India, Pakistan, and Sri Lanka) were examined in the first half of the book, and a theoretical analysis of the collective violence, particularly on the routinization of riot, and theories on "mobs" and "moral economy," were presented in the latter half of the book.

In the same year, Valentine Daniel published *Charred Lullabies: Chapters in an Anthropography of Violence* (1996). The author experienced the violence during his fieldwork on Tamil women's folk music in tea plantations. The experience made him change the topic of his PhD thesis and anti-Tamil violence became his major focus. He posed this question: "How does an anthropologist write an ethnography or...an anthropography of violence, without it becoming a pornography of violence?" (Daniel 1996: 4).

The common characteristic of the four books is their perspective in viewing collective violence as "an event which happened/could happen to ordinary citizens in India/Sri Lanka," and hence, anybody can be victim (and perhaps attacker) in the phenomenon known as a "riot." In particular, the authors on the Delhi riot such as Chakravarti, Haksar, and Das were involved in the relief and rehabilitation process or court cases, and conducted interviews, and tried to positively reinterpret the role of scholars and intellectuals at the time of large-scale violence. Their efforts to relate academic research and practice led them to work on the methodology of how the social sciences can deal with issues such as the "pain" and "suffering" of survivors, which is one of the fruitful products of the study of collective violence. At the same time, this issue led to the question of how to interpret the narratives and memories in the study of collective violence, which became one of the major issues in the area.[2]

Relationship between "Communal Riots" and Colonialism

While sociologists and social anthropologists dealt with the issue of contemporary collective violence, historians worked extensively on "riots," particularly the so-called (Hindu–Muslim) communal riots during the colonial period and at the time of Partition. Such studies not only provided rich data on the collective violence that took place during the colonial period and at the time of Partition, but were also notable in reconsidering concepts such as "communalism" and "riots." In particular, Gyanendra Pandey has written a number of interesting articles and books on the issue.

In India, it is not a new argument to point out that "communalism" is a product of colonialism. The nationalists who sought to attain independence from the British saw the communal confrontation between the Hindus and the Muslims, which was heightened during the 1920s and 1930s, as a threat to their movement, arguing that such conflict was a product of manipulation by a handful of elites. Historians of independent India inherited this perspective (Chandra 1971; Sarkar 1983).

Pandey notes that "communalism" is a form of colonialist knowledge. He points out that to use "communalism" as "tension between the [religious] communities" is unique to the Indian context. Pandey comments that it is "the unique meaning that many familiar concepts acquired in Orientalist usage in order to capture the 'Otherness' of life and politics in the 'East'" (Pandey 2006: 6–9). Such a notion of "communalism" was emphasized by colonial officers but, more interestingly, the understanding was shared by the nationalists who led the independence movement. To quote Pandey's argument,

> Communalism in the colonialist perception served to designate a pathological condition. It was, like the term "tribalism"—which has been widely employed in writings on African politics and history, and indeed "factionalism," which has been popular in western political science commentary on India since the 1960s—a statement on the *nature* of particular, "primitive" societies…. Like tribalism and factionalism, communalism is given, endemic, inborn. Like them, it denies consciousness and agency to the subjected peoples of the colonized world. (Pandey 2006: 10, emphasis in original)

While the colonialists understood communalism as the age-old, essential character of the people of India, the nationalists, by contrast, recognized communalism as of recent origin, the outcome of the economic and political inequality of conflict, and the handiwork of a handful of self-interested elite groups.

At a glance, the colonialists took an essentialist position and the nationalists took an economic and political rationalist position, and their perspectives contradicted each other. However, Pandey notes that the two shared an important view in understanding communalism. To quote him again,

> Both nationalist and colonialist accept the givenness of "communalism" as a more or less tangible phenomenon whose causes can be readily identified, and of its Other—rationalism or liberalism, secularism or nationalism, however

one chooses to put it. Both see the need of Indian society in the later colonial period, or at any rate of its "backward" sections, as one of moving from "communalism" to its Other, by means of education, political struggle, economic growth, whatever. (Pandey 2006: 12–13)

Such understanding of communalism is more salient in the description of "communal violence." Pandey points out that the British colonialist considered "natives" as "the primitive Other," and that violence as inherent in Indian history.

Such colonial understanding of "riot" shares similar characteristics with earlier studies on "crowds." In the earliest phase of study on mass panic, riots, or revolutionary movements, the subjects of such collective action were spontaneous and irrational "crowds," and collective action was seen as an "aberration" that took place as a reaction to breakdown of the social order during large-scale social and political change (Fuchs and Linkenbach 2003: 1526–31; Spencer 2003: 1565–66).

On the other hand, there is a Marxist understanding that some kind of violence is necessary during social change. Such understanding is prevalent in social history on 18th- and 19th-century Europe and the United States. Sandria Freitag tried to present a new historical interpretation of collective action, including collective violence, and stated that they were rational actions. At the same time, action by the crowds is not the marginal event in the dynamics of historical change but rather a central event (Freitag 1990: 4–5, 14).

In South Asia, the Subaltern Studies Group published a number of articles and books that most successfully applied the insights of Marxist social history. However, Spencer pointed out that even with them, collective violence, especially so-called communal violence, does not fit into such an explanatory framework. This is an important point when we consider the agency of rioters and will be discussed in the latter part of this chapter.

Relationship between Collective Violence and Party Politics

Since the 1980s and 1990s, with the rise of Hindu nationalist parties such as the BJP, incidents have emerged where political parties or large-scale organizations are involved in collective violence and attempt to take advantage of them, the largest being the Ayodhya incident. The frequency of such violence led scholars to focus on the "communal riot" as "a means of politics" in contemporary South Asia. To be specific, Paul Brass and other political scientists tried to analyze the routinized riots in specific states or towns, and the involvement of political parties or large-scale ethnic and religious organizations in the incidents.

In 1997, Paul Brass published *Theft of an Idol*, which analyzed several incidents in Uttar Pradesh. He tried to illustrate how communal violence took place in local district towns in India with a focus on the local politics and police. He took the approach of reading the riot as a "text" in a Foucauldian way but then tried to analyze "who the culprit was." Although I find the use of these two methodologies at the same time theoretically contradictory, the work illustrates how police and local politicians are involved in the violence and shows that they can be a factor in facilitating and preventing riots (Brass 1997).

Brass argued that there is an "institutionalized riot system" in some towns in India—an informal network that can exaggerate trivial, everyday incidents and place them into the communal discourse, allowing them to escalate into communal violence. In this system, political parties such as the BJP or large-scale organizations such as the Rashtriya Swayamsevak Sangh (RSS) are involved. He advanced this argument in his next book, *The Production of Hindu–Muslim Violence in Contemporary India* (Brass 2003: 32). Here, he raised the question: "How is it that riots persist?" and tried to explain it by taking the functional approach that "they are functionally useful to a wide array of individuals, groups, parties and the state authorities" (Brass 2003: 33–34).

Brass' work contributed to overcoming the understanding of communal riots in the context of barbarity or primordialism, and presented a different perspective. In particular, the descriptions of local politicians and police officers in terms of involvement with the violence contributed to the understanding of how riots took place in the local towns of India, and can be regarded as a good reference in terms of the importance of politics in the emergence of collective violence in India. On the other hand, his argument on the "institutionalized riot system" cannot be applied to all towns where riots take place in India, and hence, there is a problem with generalizing this argument and a need for further elaboration.

At the same time, studies by Ashutosh Varshney and Ian Wilkinson on "communal riots" in India emerged, where they compiled a dataset on "communal violence" in India from 1950–1995 based on newspaper articles. Based on the dataset, Varshney tried to present an overall picture and the trends of violence, such as that most riots took place in urban rather than rural areas, and that there were riot-prone states or towns. Based on the findings, Varshney compared riot-prone towns and peaceful towns in India, and tried to explain the factors that caused this difference. His conclusion was that interethnic or intercommunal, ethnic, civic engagement was the key factor in preventing violence (Varshney 2002: 111, 281).

While Brass and Varshney focused on town-level analysis, Wilkinson focused on party politics at the state level. He stated that when the minority (Muslim) vote was decisive in state politics, the government was active in preventing riots, but if not, the ruling party did not take preventive action or, rather, instigated the riots. By using a dataset from 1950 to 1995, he tried to explain such "electoral incentives" for Hindu–Muslim violence (Wilkinson 2004: 94–96, 137, 169–71).

Varshney and Wilkinson's analyses based on the dataset has proven some of the most important characteristics of collective violence in contemporary India. For example, the number of deaths by communal violence is much higher in urban areas than in rural areas. Less than four percent of total deaths from violence in India take place in rural areas (Varshney 2002: 95–96).

Their data based on statistics tend to focus more on small-scale rather than large-scale violence. For example, because they have limited the scope of their study to "Hindu–Muslim communal riots," some of the largest incidents of violence in independent India have not been included, such as the anti-Sikh riots in Delhi in 1984 and the Nellie riot in 1983. Although the Nellie incident involved the Hindu and Muslim communities, it was not included, perhaps because their focus was on riots that are of relevance to Hindu nationalism. Similarly, the Gujarat incident was not included since it took place after 1995. Hence, the Bhagalpur riot was the only incident with a death toll of more than 1,000 to be included in their data. Thus, although their studies have been successful in showing certain characteristics of collective violence in India, unfortunately, the Nellie incident, a major focus of this book, does not fit into the framework they have provided.

Varshney and Wilkinson have developed notable arguments and theories on collective violence that differ from one another, although their arguments are based on the same data. However, they do appear to share a basic understanding of the "riot," with the intervention of political parties or large-scale organizations as definitive of the "Hindu–Muslim communal riot," and it being routinized violence in specific towns and states in India. They thereby contribute to creating this type of image in the discipline of political science. This also shares similarity with Brass' understanding on communal violence. I would rather point out that Brass' study has had a substantial impact in understanding the religious riot in political science (particularly in the US).

These theories and arguments on "riots" should be highly valued for their contribution in overcoming the stereotype that the violence between the Hindus and the Muslims was rooted in their historical confrontation and primordial identity, and showing the importance of politics in the analysis of collective violence. At the same time, their emphasis on the intervention and manipulation by politicians and the police has led to the argument that collective violence is always "produced" (to borrow Brass' term), and that riot participants are *goonda* and criminal groups or "mobs" who are merely used by politicians like puppets.

Although it is true that these types of incidents often take place in India, there have been other types of collective violence as well. The violence that took place during the Partition was larger in scale, and although the politicians tried to intervene and control it in the beginning, the violence spread beyond their expectations and became uncontrollable even with the force of the army and police, as Brass too notes (Brass 2003: 31). In such instances, the riot participants were not necessarily *goonda*s or criminal groups, with "ordinary people" too participating. The Nellie incident in Assam in 1983 was one such incident that does not fit into the model of a "Hindu–Muslim communal riot" controlled by political parties and large-scale organizations. What I try to focus on in the study of the Nellie massacre is the perspective of ordinary people's participation in a riot, which has been overlooked in the studies. Let us turn to the issues of participation by the ordinary people in collective violence and the agency of rioters.

Agency of Rioters

The lack of study of participants in collective riots is not unique to political science. In *Mirrors of Violence*, published in 1990, Veena Das states, "[o]ne of the greatest lacunae in our understanding of collective action, including collective violence, is the lack of an organized body of empirical knowledge on these issues" (Das 1990: 28). The lack of data on the participants is caused by methodological difficulty because interviewing them is considerably difficult—in most cases, almost impossible.

Let us take a look at the traditional perspectives of theories on crowds. In studies of mass psychology on crowds such as by Le Bon and Muscovici, the perception of a crowd is illustrated as emotional, capricious, temperamental, and flighty (Das 1990: 26; Moscovici 1985). They are recognized as a passive group of people who are mobilized by active leaders and moved to action by unconscious urges, and thus, the reason for their participation in the violence has rarely been questioned.

On the other hand, there is a view that crowds choose to participate in collective action by rational choice. Thompson (1971) tried to explain the collective action by English crowds in food riots in the 18th century by using the concept of moral economy. His analysis was that those who took part in the food riots reformulated the traditional rights in a new moral economy, having faced the transition of the traditional moral economy where all the members of the community were secured their existence, to the emergence of a new order in the modernized system (Thompson 1971: 78). However, Das argues that such a view on the rational crowd seems directly opposed to the kinds of crowds involved in collective violence in contemporary South Asia (Das 1990: 27).

Similarly, Spencer argues that such arguments by Thompson and others tend to concentrate on this kind of violence, grain riots or destruction of machinery, which fit most readily into the template of putative social revolution (Spencer 2003: 1568–69). In the South Asian context, the scholars of the Subaltern Studies Group are notable in applying such an approach to cases in India. The founder of the group, Ranajit Guha, focused on peasant insurgency in the colonial period and analyzed that their perspectives are completely different from that of the colonizers (Guha 1983a). However, Spencer points out that the so-called communal violence in South Asia does not suit this explanatory framework, because its distinguishing feature is rarely the powerless attacking the powerful, or the poor taking on the powers that be. The typical feature of the revolutionary crowds is that the poor or the powerless challenge the powerful. However, Spencer states, "[c]ommunal violence, especially, in the colonial and immediately post-colonial period, most often involves sections of the urban poor attacking each other" (Spencer 2003: 1569).

Gyanendra Pandey, one of the leading historians in the Subaltern Studies Group, has analyzed the relationship between colonialism and the concept of communal riots. Later on, in a paper on the Bhagalpur riot in Bihar, which took place in 1989, he pointed out that the incident was of a different character compared to earlier ones. Based on his experience of visiting the site of the violence with a civil society group, he stated,

> Sectarian violence in the 1980s appears to have taken on new and increasingly horrifying forms. Recent strife between people belonging to different religious denominations has not been restricted to pitched battles on the streets or cloak-and-dagger attacks and murders in side lanes, which were the chief markers of earlier riots. The worst instances of recent violence have amounted to pogroms, organized massacres in which large crowds of hundreds, thousands, and even, in places, tens of thousands have attacked the houses and property and lives of small, isolated, and previously identified members of the "other" community. (Pandey 1992: 46)

Moreover, he stated that in this incident, the influence of the violent slogans and demands of organizations like the Vishwa Hindu Parishad was not only limited to the moment of the riot, but became widely accepted and part of a popular dogma (Pandey 1992: 42).

At the same time, what Pandey emphasized was that the statement of complex, long-term historical processes leaves little room for human agency and human responsibility. The economic interests, conflicts over land, and control by the elite leave little room for the emotions of people, for feelings and perceptions—in a word, little room for agency (Pandey 1992: 40–41). In order to overcome such limits, there have been attempts by scholars such as Veena Das to focus on the suffering and pain of the survivors, as noted earlier in this chapter.[3] However, as has been argued, there are very few studies on the agency of riot participants.

Beth Roy studied the agency of riot participants by taking the case of a rural riot in former East Pakistan. Roy interviewed both the attackers and the victims of the riot, and concluded that the villagers chose to riot through a rational decision-making process, although passion and circumstance figured in their decisions (Roy 1994: 137). The incident was triggered by a banal conflict that a cow owned by a Muslim peasant had eaten a Hindu neighbor's plants. There are no archival records on this issue, and thus, Roy's research relied solely on interviews of the villagers, and she reconstructed the incident in order to analyze what drove the villagers to riot. One thing that Roy emphasized was that there had been no intervention by "outside organizers," at least according to the villagers' accounts. In analyses of communal violence, there are often cases where "outside agitators" controlled the "ignorant and innocent villagers." However, in this case, there was no involvement of outside forces, and hence, Roy focused on the decision making of the local people (Roy 1994: 133–34).

Roy referred to Gramsci, who is also often quoted by the Subaltern Studies Group. She argued that as pointed out by Gramsci, culture was controlled by those in power and produced a hegemonic, or dominating, philosophy. However, the powerless are also capable of exercising will and creativity in shaping their world. She tried to explore the way people who were relatively powerless took power, or, more accurately, negotiated it, within the limitations of institutional arrangements they could not effectively challenge. Such action is limited, as it cannot effectively challenge the framework, but it leads to the understanding of the recognition of the powerless before and during the collective violence (Roy 1994: 131–32).

Based on this assumption, Roy presented one hypothesis on communalism, or more precisely, communal violence: "People act out a particular drama, attempting to renegotiate rights and powers in forms limited and distorted by oppression." She further argued that the particular frame in which they engaged in meaningful struggles was constituted by unequal power relations that constrained the spaces within which they could move towards well-being (Roy 1994: 132).

Her findings suggest that in the exercise of agency, participants of collective violence do not have many options, and that these are often limited by power-holders. The fact that the repertoire of collective actions available to a population is limited has been pointed out in earlier studies (Tilly 1978: 151). However, an important point raised in Roy's study is that it is essential to understand how the options available to riot participants are perceived, especially in rural areas. The perceptions of rural peasants based on their everyday experiences are different from those of the urban middle class, and the range of collective actions available to them is more limited than we assume. Thus, the main focus in a study of the agency of rioters would be to examine the process of how people, individually or collectively, perceive and analyze the situation, and choose to riot under certain circumstances.

Some key conditions for people to make the decision to participate in riots are: (1) The distinction between enemy and "us" is demarcated along ethnic lines. These are mainly defined by national/ethnic/religious movements preceding the disturbance. In terms of the Hindu–Muslim "communal riots," this refers to the right-wing Hindu nationalism movement. In terms of the Nellie incident, it was the antiforeigner movement. (2) Small-scale incidents against members of the community have already taken place, and people have felt acute threats to their security. Regarding the Nellie incident, there were reports of the Tiwa children being killed, and people felt the need to conduct a preemptive attack to prevent the possible attack. A sense of insecurity can legitimize action. For those taking advantage of the situation, this can be used as an excuse to counter the arguments of those opposing violent actions. (3) People know that, for certain reasons the law enforcement agencies would not work against them.

The last point needs some explanation. In most cases of collective violence in contemporary South Asia, either the government is sympathetic to the movement or some top politicians are involved in the incident. Regarding the Nellie incident, however, the Congress government did not collaborate with the attackers or the All Assam Students' Union (AASU). Rather, it confronted the student leaders.

At the time, Assam was under President's rule and the state government had been dissolved. Thus, it was the Government of India (GOI) led by the Congress that had the power and authority to ensure security in the state. Unlike the anti-Sikh violence in Delhi in 1984, during which the Congress encouraged (or perhaps led) the rioters to attack the Sikhs, this time, it was keen to mobilize security for the Muslims (their solid vote bank), and conduct a State Legislative Assembly election without problems. The antiforeigner movement was led by the AASU and regional parties, who were competing with the Congress for state power. The government thus tried its best to suppress the boycott. In fact, the GOI deployed the Central Reserve Police Force (CRPF), paramilitary forces, and police from other states in order to enforce the state election.

The Congress's priority was to take power in the state. It was aware that violence would erupt if it forced an election without revising the electoral rolls. In fact, the AASU declared a boycott of the election, but this provided an opportunity for the Congress to gain a majority in the State Legislative Assembly and establish government. The Congress took it as a good chance, and in order to hold the election, provided extra deployment of police and security forces in poll booths and guards for election candidates.

It was clear at the time that the AASU was supported by the masses in Assam, and that it would try to stop the election from being held by force, which would lead to widespread violence. The Congress underestimated the AASU's influence, and at the same time, did not pay attention to the security of the Muslims and other party supporters who were potential targets of violence. Moreover, at the time, Assam state police personnel also supported the AASU and the movement, and did not work actively to prevent the violence. Instead, many collaborated with AASU supporters and joined in the attacks. In the case of the Nellie incident, there were rumors that the police had lent a hand in the attack, or had at least helped them obtain arms and ammunitions. Thus, when violence erupted in many parts of Assam due to the election boycott, the police and security personnel failed to control the situation. The local police did not take effective action to stop the killings until the arrival of the CRPF.

Understanding the complexity of this situation will enable us to understand the uniqueness of the Nellie incident. The confrontation between the GOI and the AASU, particularly during the State Legislative Assembly election, paralyzed law enforcement agencies and created a vacuum of power, leaving room for the local peasants to exercise their agency during the disturbance. This marks the distinguishing character of the Nellie incident.

Memory of Violence and Identity

In order to understand and analyze narratives of the violence, I noticed the importance of taking into account the theories on "memory" for two reasons. One is that what the victims and the attackers, as well as those involved in the incident, share about a large-scale incident is not only their first-hand experience, but also second-hand information, such as newspaper reports and stories they hear from family members, relatives, and neighbors. Thus, we need to take into consideration the social or collective aspects of such memory. The second point is that memories of violence are very closely connected with collective identity. In particular, regarding ethnic or religious violence, the victims are attacked simply because they belong to certain ethnic or religious groups. Thus, their narratives on the incident, and particularly regarding who the enemies were, are deeply related to the collective identity that develops after the incident.

To gain some clarity on the matter, it would be useful to take a look at the arguments on collective memory advanced by Halbwachs (1992). According to this scholar, there are two types of memory: biographical memory and historical memory. The former is memory of events that we have personally experienced in the past, and the latter is memorized only through written and other types of records, such as documents and photography. Halbwachs calls the latter "collective memory" or "social memory." In collective memory, the person does not directly participate in the events, and the past is stored and interpreted by social institutions.

Such distinction between biographical memory and social memory is not clear in the case of the narratives of riot participants and survivors. Most of the villagers in the Nellie area experienced the violence directly, and people tend to believe that their narratives are their biographical memory. However, when a certain set of stories about the incident gained popularity and when they were communicated to and shared with members of the group who were not directly involved in it, we can see the establishment of a collective memory.

Such phenomenon is presently visible in the case of the Nellie incident. When I conducted interviews with the attackers, mostly the Tiwas, and the victims, contrary to my expectations, the attackers were more vocal than the victims in stating the reason for their attacks. Moreover, their narratives are closely related with the present political status and identity formation that emerged during the autonomous movement. In order to understand this, it helps to focus on the arguments on construction of collective identity and its relation with violence in history.

It is argued that history is essential in the formation of a collective identity (a nation, ethnic group, or community). Anderson explains that as a person needs his own biography, so do nations, in order to "forget" the past division within the community and prove the continuity (Anderson 1983: 204–05). Narratives on violence in particular (for example, war, riot, or massacre) constitute an important part of the development of national, ethnic, or communal identity. Gyanendra Pandey, in his book on violence during the Partition, states as follows.

> It is my argument that in the history of any society, narratives of particular experiences of violence go towards making the "community" and the subject of history. The discipline of history still proceeds on the assumption of a

fixed subject—society, nation, state, community, locality, whatever it might be—and a largely pre-determined course of human development or transformation. However, the agent and locus of history is hardly pre-designated. Rather, accounts of history, shared experiences in the past, serve to constitute and these, their extent and their boundaries. In the instance at hand, I shall suggest, violence too becomes a language that constitutes—and reconstitutes—the subject. (Pandey 2001: 4)

In narrating experiences of incidents of violence, people develop their "common memory" and construct the "we" and "the Other." These narratives emphasize how they faced tremendous difficulties, and how the enemy carried out the cruel attacks. In this process they define who the enemy—"the Other"—was and at the same time construct the "us." It is often the case that "we" are posited as victims and "the Other" as the perpetrator of violence. In this manner, a narrative of particular violence becomes an important part of nationalism.

Another important argument made by Halbwachs is that the past is a social construction mainly, if not wholly, shaped by the concerns of the present. This is called the "presentist approach," and Halbwachs was the first sociologist to stress this point. In other words, our conceptions of the past are affected by the mental images we employ to solve present problems, so that collective memory is essentially a reconstruction of the past. Although this too-pronounced presentism has been modified by works of later scholars, this approach remains the basic starting point in analyzing memory. Viewed thus, present interviews on violence reveal more about the present state of things than of the past.

This means that the interviews on the Nellie incident will lead to the analysis of the present situation of the survivors and the attackers in the violence. This shows the possibility of research not only on the past but also the effects of the incident. At the same time, it has been more than 20 years since the incident, and thus the question arises whether the interviewees' answers can be taken as a testimony on the past or a memory, which can include the things that did not take place. In order to answer this question, I used two methods in analyzing the incident based on the interviews. One was to refer to written records such as police reports and inquiry commission reports and compare them with the narratives, analyzing things that could be taken as facts. This method can be seen mainly in Chapters 3 and 4, where I analyze the relationship between the student leaders and the attackers in the Nellie incident.

Another method was to focus on the difference in perspective between the student leaders and attackers, as well as survivors. The focus here was to analyze how such differences emerged among groups experiencing the same violence yet from completely different positions, and how their narratives differed from one another. Thus, it was not necessary to specify facts using this method; it was important to analyze what people believed. This method can be seen in Chapter 6 and has been partly applied in Chapter 5.

Before analyzing narratives of the Nellie incident, however, I would like to do an overall analysis of the history of the Assamese nationalist movement, which led to the antiforeigner movement in the 1970s and 1980s. Assam hosts a large number of immigrant populations, especially the Muslims, due to the immigration policies of the British government. However, a sizeable Muslim population does not necessarily lead to xenophobia. In fact, there was an anti-immigrant sentiment in Assam until the 1970s, but directed towards middle-class Bengalis, who are mostly Hindu. It is necessary to analyze how the antiforeigner movement targeted the Muslims in relation to the political change in Assam at the time, notably with the decline of the Congress and the emergence of regional parties. I explain this background in the following chapter.

Notes

1. For example, Asghar Ali Engineer had published a number of articles even earlier. See Engineer (1984).
2. For example, see the concluding chapter of Butalia (1998) on the argument of memories. Also, regarding the relationship between history, memory, and violence, see Pandey (2001) and Amin (1995).
3. See Kleinman, Das and Lock (1997), Das et al. (2000), and Das et al. (2001).

3

Locating the Antiforeigner Movement in the Context of Assamese Nationalism

Context of Assamese Nationalist Movement: The Colonial Period

The root of the anti-immigrant reactions by the Assamese people can be traced to the large-scale immigration of people from outside the state, such as the middle-class Bengalis, the Muslims of East Bengal origin, and tea-garden laborers, which took place during the colonial period. However, immigration by itself does not abruptly ignite a mass-mobilized movement. In this chapter, I examine how and why the antiforeigner movement took place in Assam during this period by exploring the broader socioeconomic milieu and political history.

At the outset, I will go through the historical context of the nationalist aspirations in Assam. The nationalist movement in Assam started as a reaction towards the imposition of Bengali language and the dominance of the Bengali-speaking, middle-class people in the colonial administration of the region. It is imperative to scrutinize such historical context to understand the oppositions and counterarguments from the middle-class Bengali media and public opinion to the antiforeigner movement. The scarcity of land and the displacement of the marginal communities called tribes, who are the original inhabitants of the area, emerged as an issue in this period.

Moreover, the period of the antiforeigner movement saw a sweeping political change where the dominance of the Congress party came to an end and the Janata party assumed power in the center. Together with the fall of the Congress, nationalist movements in regions like Punjab emerged with strong support from the people. The antiforeigner movement in Assam also emerged in this context of the rise in aspirations of the people of the region. Considering these circumstances will help us understand more clearly why a significant movement took place in Assam, and why the target of the movement became the "illegal immigrants and foreigners."

The large-scale influx of immigrants to Assam took place during the colonial period. The British officers regarded the former Ahom officials not suitable for colonial administration, and encouraged immigration in order to manage the colonial administration and to introduce modern industry in Assam. The immigrants played an important role in the incorporation of Assam into the colonial political system and economic structure. At first, the middle-class Bengalis who already had experience in colonial administration were imported from Sylhet, Dhaka, and Mymensingh as colonial functionaries (Nag 1990: 34–37).

The immigration was directed to meet the needs of not only the administration, but also of other sectors. As a result, British colonization brought about a change in the political, economic, and social structures in Assam. In the case of tea plantations, which became a major colonial industry in Assam, the tribes from Orissa and Bihar were brought to work as laborers.

In addition to the administration-sponsored officials and plantation workers, there were other economic migrants such as the Marwaris who came from the Indian mainland. The Marwaris acted as moneychangers, bankers, and dealers in various commodities, particularly rice and grains. They monopolized almost the whole trade and commerce of Assam and played an important role in opening the state to the Indian market. Even agriculture, the predominant economic sector in the region, was commercialized under the name of modernization in order to increase colonial revenue. Thus, the large-scale immigration of the Muslim peasants from East Bengal was encouraged and they were successful in producing cash crops (Nag 1990: 39–41).

Initially the Assamese people, who owned enough land and produced sufficient crops for their own needs, found it difficult to adjust to the changes in society. To a great extent, the socioeconomic and political changes in the region were related to one crucial process that was happening unabated—land alienation of the Assamese people. In addition to it, when they sought employment in the modern sector they had to experience stiff competition with the immigrants. In this context, the Assamese national sentiment took place in the form of opposition to the immigrants and their dominance over the land of the indigenous people. The first major reaction by the Assamese people, the demand for the adoption of Assamese as the language of administration, occurred in response to the Bengali dominance in administration.

Language as a Symbol of Distinct Identity

The consciousness of a distinct Assamese nationality began symbolically with the affection of their language and identity. British occupation brought increased interaction with Bengali society. As noted, the British administration promoted the immigration of an educated section of Bengali officers to Assam. Along with this action, Bengali language was introduced as a medium of revenue administration and education in schools. The step was aided by the Bengalis' openness to change.

On encountering the British civilization, Bengali society experienced substantial transformation until the time Assam was colonized, and in the cultural realm, it took the form of the "Bengali Renaissance." As a consequence, Bengali culture came to be recognized as the most "advanced" among the native cultures in India, and accordingly institutes for higher education were established in Bengal in order to produce colonial administrative staff. Thus, the Assamese found themselves to be latecomers to the modernizing society in colonial India. To catch up with the civilizing process and counter the hegemony of Bengal, the Assamese not only promoted their language and culture but also emphasized their difference with the Bengalis.

As a first step to achieve this objective, a memorandum was submitted to Moffat Mills by Anandaram Dekhiyal Phukan. This act is widely cited as the first attempt to reinstate the Assamese language to its "right" status (Misra 2001: 19). In the memorandum, Dekhiyal Phukan—who was born to a Brahmin landowning family, educated in the Hindu College of Calcutta, and later became a government servant—categorically stated that even though a number of vernacular schools had been established in Assam, instruction in these schools was "imparted in a foreign language, viz., the Bengalee, which is but imperfectly understood by the teachers themselves, not to speak of the pupils" (Baruah 1999: 59; Guha 1977: 22). With the help of the American Baptist Mission, a section of the Assamese people lodged a complaint on the issue, and Assamese was introduced as the language of courts and schools, under the Bengal Government Order of April 19, 1873 (Guha 1977: 22; Nag 1990: 49–59).

Simultaneously, there were moves to form organizations for the promotion of Assamese language and literature. Accordingly, in 1872 the Assamese Literary Society was formed in Calcutta at the initiative of the Assamese residents in the city, including students who were studying at the prestigious Presidency College. In 1888, the Asamiya Bhasa Unnati Sadhani Samiti was formed, again by Assamese middle-class students in Calcutta. Here, the prime objective was to establish a standard language throughout Assam. Many contemporary observers view the formation of these literary organizations as the emergence of modern political consciousness in Assam (Guha 1977: 24; Misra 2001: 19–26; Nag 1990: 113–16).

The influence of Bengali culture at that time was very strong. As noted, students studying in Calcutta played a pioneering role not only in establishing these literary organizations to which many middle-class Assamese extended their support, but also in lighting the flame of Assamese nationality. Being the capital of British India at the time, Calcutta was the nerve center of cultural activity; hence the emergence of the modern literary movement was called the "Bengali Renaissance." Scholars such as Amalendu Guha and Sajal Nag have pointed out these aspects (Guha 1977: 21–24; Nag 1990: 79). Sanjib Baruah too concedes this point but also emphasizes the importance of the feeling of resentment prevalent among the Assamese towards Bengali dominance (Baruah 1999: 60). Thus, it is evident from such observations that Assamese nationality in the early colonial period was more or less stimulated by the encounter with Bengalis and their culture, with the strong feeling of resentment towards their political, economic, and social dominance in the Assamese people's own land.

Immigrants, Sense of "Our Land," and Debates over the Line System

In the early 1900s, pressure on land caused by the presence of a large number of Bengali peasants became the main political issue in Assam. As noted earlier, British colonial officers promoted large-scale migration from Bengal to Assam in order to deal with the problem of land scarcity in Bengal and to increase land revenue in Assam. The process began in the late 19th century, but large-scale population movement occurred from the 1900s onwards (Baruah 1999: 55–57). Indeed, in the 1931 census, C. S. Mullan, superintendent of census operations in Assam, had made a prediction about the possible impact of the large presence of the immigrants, especially that of Bengali Muslims, on the land of Assam. Mullan's prediction was one of the most quoted phrases at the time of the antiforeigner movement. I quote:

> Probably the most important event in the province during the last twenty-five years…has been the invasion of a vast horde of land-hungry Bengali immigrants, mostly Muslims, from the districts of Eastern Bengal and in particular from Mymensingh….
>
> It is sad but by no means improbable that in another thirty years Sibsagar District will be the only part of Assam in which an Assamese will find himself at home. (Census of India, 1931, Volume 3, Assam)

The number of immigrants kept increasing in the 1930s, and there emerged a growing dissatisfaction and fear against the Muslim immigrants among the Assamese people. The matter reached its peak in the mid-1930s when the Assamese began to feel the pressure of the Muslim peasants with regard to their rights over land.

In the mid-1930s, there was a controversy between the Hindus and the Muslims over the Line System and immigration policy. And almost at the same time, the British government introduced provincial autonomy and an election was held for the State Legislative Assembly under a separate electorate. Here, the Indian National Congress and the Muslim League emerged as prominent political parties in the Assembly, and the controversy over the Line System occurred between these two parties (Kar 1997: 35–38).

The Line System was first proposed in 1916 and introduced in 1920 with a view to protect the local people from the land pressure caused by the presence of the Bengali Muslim peasants. The idea was to segregate the land reserved for the local people and that reserved for the exclusive settlement of the immigrants. Since the introduction of the system, local people who wanted to reserve the land for the Assamese complained of the inefficiency of the system and demanded that it be strengthened, while the Muslims demanded its abolition. Expectedly, the former demand was represented by the Congress, and the latter by the Muslim League in the State Legislative Assembly, and debates arose over several resolutions raised by both the parties (Guha 1977: 208–10, 256–63; Kar 1997: 8–20, 86–92; Nag 1990: 125–30).

In the 1940s, the immigration policy was carried out by the Muslim League ministry led by Saadulla. Particularly in 1942 during his fourth ministry, the Government of India's (GOI) "Grow More Food" scheme was put into operation, and under this policy Saadulla tried to increase the land settlement of the migrants. The policy was criticized by the Congress, and even the Viceroy during his visit to Assam stated that it actually meant "Grow More Muslims" policy (Kar 1997: 8–20, 86–92; Nag 1991: 125–30). Thus, the policy resulted in deprivation of the Assamese people's sources of livelihood as they were not provided with a viable alternative to improve their condition.

Due to the controversy over the Line System and immigration policy, and for various reasons, the period saw the rise to prominence of a sense of "our land" among a section of the Assamese people. Those people who saw immigrants as a "threat" to Assam drew a line between the indigenous and immigrant communities, based on the idea of colonization of Assam. The descendants of the population who started to live in Assam before the British occupation were regarded as "local, indigenous" people, while those who started to live in Assam after colonization were seen as "immigrants" even if they were born in Assam. The important point here is that the dichotomy still has significant meaning in present Assamese society (Baruah 1999: 18). For the first time, land and immigration became closely linked, and hence the distinction between the local and immigrant communities became important.

Partition and the Emergence of Assam State

In 1946, the issue of immigration and Hindu–Muslim confrontation saw a major turn, and the communal situation became more tense than anything previously experienced. In the year that the Cabinet Mission Plan was proposed, Assam was grouped with East Bengal and it was proposed that it be transferred to Pakistan. Initially, the leaders of the All India Congress Committee opposed the move, but later on compromised with the plan in order to expedite the process of independence.

However, the leaders of the Assam Pradesh Congress Committee led by Gopinath Bordoloi filed a complaint against this plan. Backed by M. K. Gandhi, they led a massive campaign against the transfer of Assam to Pakistan. To resolve the matter, it was decided that a referendum would be held in the Sylhet District (a district bordering East Bengal, with a predominantly Bengali-Muslim population) and the rest of Assam would remain in India. The Assam Pradesh Congress Committee, which always wanted to deter the immigration from Bengal, welcomed the partition of Sylhet from Assam and was ready to accept the result of the referendum. This compromise formula sealed the fate of Sylhet and it was transferred to Pakistan in 1947 (Chakrabarty 2002: 333–35; Guha 1977: 309–20; Kar 1997: 40).

Compared to the language problem in the 19th century, the campaign against the grouping plan successfully mobilized the masses and for the first time created a wider social tension among many sections of the people in Assam. Commenting on the situation, Amalendu Guha states, "Never was the communal situation in Assam so tense as in the last year of the British rule" (Guha 1977: 315–20; Nag 1990: 145–56).

However, after the partition and the independence of India, most of the Bengali Muslim peasants remained in Assam, adopted Assamese as their mother tongue, and declared themselves as Assamese speaking to the census enumerators. Thus, the issue of religion and hostility towards the Muslims cooled down considerably.

From the Linguistic Movements to the Antiforeigner Movement: The Postcolonial Period

The partition and independence of India brought about major changes in Assam's polity. First of all, the Assamese-speaking population became the majority in Assam for the first time since colonization. As a result of the referendum, the Sylhet District was separated from Assam and transferred to Pakistan. Sylhet was a densely populated district and its population comprised nearly 30 percent of Assam's population, with more than 90 percent of the population Bengali-speaking (Census of India 1931). But with the transfer of Sylhet, the percentage of the Assamese population in the state increased from 30 percent to 56 percent (Census of India 1951).

Second, the Partition and the accompanying violence between the Hindus and the Muslims triggered a large-scale influx of refugees. Prior to Partition, in 1946, there was a series of riots and mass killings in neighboring Bengal. In the process, many Hindus and Muslims had become refugees and crossed the border—the Hindus into India and the Muslims into East Pakistan. It has been said that there were many refugees from Sylhet. The 1951 census revealed that there were 275,455 Bengali Hindus who crossed the border into India before and after Partition (Census of India 1951).

Third, with the formalization of the Partition, the East Bengal region was transformed into East Pakistan and became a separate nation-state from India, making the residents there "foreigners." Thus, before independence, the movement of people from the area was regarded as interprovincial migration, as Sylhet then was part of the same political unit as the rest of India. However, after Partition, the Muslim migrants became "illegal immigrants" or "foreigners," whereas the Hindus were regarded as "refugees." What added to the problem was that even in the post-Partition period, migration from East Pakistan into India continued unabated. In particular, at the time of the Bangladesh war of liberation, there was a large-scale movement of population from that country into India.

In the postindependence period, it is unknown whether the immigrants were Hindus or Muslims because there are no official statistics. Scholars like Susanta Krishna Dass state that it was the Hindus who crossed the border after Partition, while Weiner points out the abnormal increase of the Muslim population in the census of India from 1951 to 1971 (Dass 1980: 850–59; Weiner 1983: 285–86). In a recent research conducted by scholars in Assam, it has been stated that from 1951 to 1991, there were two million illegal immigrants in India from East Pakistan or Bangladesh (Goswami et al. 2002).

Language as a Boundary of Ethnic Communities: The Demand for the Official Language of the State of Assam

In the postindependence period, the demand for the recognition of Assamese as the official language became a central issue in Assam. The Asam Sahitya Sabha, the most influential social organization in Assam, under the leadership of Ambikagiri Roy Choudhury raised the demand as early as 1950 (Dutt 1953: 12–13). However, it was not until the end of the 1950s that the demand was taken serious note of by the State Legislative Assembly. The Assam Pradesh Congress Committee passed a resolution on April 24, 1960 that Assamese should be declared as the official language of the state. Following this resolution, the Assam Official Language Bill was passed in the legislative assembly on October 24, 1960 (Goswami 1997: 50–54; *The Assam Official Language Act, 1960*).

During this period, the move for the declaration of the official language met with severe opposition from the Bengali and indigenous tribal communities, particularly from Cachar and the various hill districts in the state, and in June and July 1960 there was a series of violent incidents among different linguistic and ethnic communities. The tense situation continued even after the bill was passed in the Assembly. The severest opposition came from the Bengali community in Cachar and on May 19, 1961, there was a violent incident in Silchar (a major town in Cachar) in which eight persons were killed in police firing against the satyagrahis of the strike. In order to contain the situation, the Union Home Minister Lal Bahadur Shastri came to Cachar for mediation and proposed the amendment of the Act. The Assembly accepted the formula offered by Shastri and passed the amendment to the Language Bill on October 7, 1961 (Goswami 1997: 57, 64–66; Statement of Shri Lal Bahadur Shastri 1961).

At that time, the promoters of the Assamese language defined the Bengali Hindus as a "threat." As stated earlier in this chapter, there was a predominance of the Bengali Hindus in the modern sector of employment in the colonial period. The Bengali Hindu's presence in the administrative services was still significant in the 1950s, and there was dissatisfaction among the Assamese people due to the Bengali dominance. It was articulated during the process of the demand for the official language bill and the disturbances that followed the passing of the bill.

The strong demand for the official language bill by the Asam Sahitya Sabha and other sections of the Assamese society was viewed as an oppressive measure by the indigenous tribes in Assam, especially those in the hill areas. This accelerated a demand for a separate hill state by the hill tribes.

In 1969, Meghalaya was created as an autonomous state within the state of Assam, comprising the United Khasi–Jaintia Hills District and the Garo Hills District. In 1972, it led to the creation of the states of Meghalaya, Manipur, and Tripura. At the same time, the Mizo Hills, the former Lushai Hills, was elevated to a union territory, along with the North-East Frontier Agency.

It is important to note that at this time the Assamese nationalist movement had an assimilative tendency to impose the Assamese language on all the communities in Assam. This continued until the mid-1970s, when the Gauhati University decided to introduce Assamese as the language of education in the colleges under its jurisdiction. The decision brought about fierce opposition again from the Bengali community in Cachar. However, at the end of the 1970s, the nationalist movement in Assam took a drastic turn in the opposite direction.

The Antiforeigner Movement

By the end of the 1970s, there was a major transformation in the political scenario of Assam. Until this time, the Assamese language was established as the official language in the state and as a medium of instruction at the Gauhati University. Although there were still continuing debates on language, the center of focus shifted to the issue of foreign nationals.

It has been pointed out that there was a large influx of Bengali Muslim peasants from erstwhile East Pakistan, and present-day Bangladesh. As shown earlier in this chapter, this process had spawned anxiety in colonial times too. But this time, the situation acquired a different complexion as the East Bengal region became part of a foreign country, and the immigration problem could no longer be viewed as an interstate population movement but a transnational movement.

The problem had been raised several times earlier, but the movement received momentum only when the by-election to the Lok Sabha in the Mangaldoi parliamentary constituency was announced. During this time, it was found that the number of voters had gone up phenomenally. Soon after, the All Assam Students' Union (AASU) demanded that the election be postponed and the names of foreign nationals be deleted from the electoral rolls.

To intensify their demand, in August 1979, the AASU coordinated with the Asam Sahitya Sabha, some regional political parties, and a youth organization, and formed an umbrella organization called the All Assam Gana Sangram Parishad (AAGSP). Their objectives were to detect the names of foreigners in the electoral rolls, delete them from the rolls, and deport the subjects from Assam.

For the AASU, the organizers of the movement, the threat this time was the presence of "foreigners," unlike in the 1960s when the threat had come from the cultural domination of the "Bengali Hindus" and the strategy adopted had been the introduction of one's own national language (Assamese) to counter the threat of the cultural "Other." This time, however, the threat came from the large influx of "foreigners" from across the international border. To highlight the danger posed to the demographic structure of the state, the organizers of the movement came up with a number of pamphlets on the sharp increase in the rate of the population based on census figures. In one of their most widely distributed pamphlets, "Voice of AASU: Mass Upheaval in Assam," they estimated that there were 4.5 million foreigners in the state (AASU 1980a: 2). Taking into account that the population of the state of Assam was 14,625,152 as per the 1971 census, it undeniably was a considerable number.

The AASU and AAGSP leaders were careful to avoid the criticism of being communal. Hence they took careful steps to clearly define who the "foreigners" were and projected the problem not simply as a local or regional problem but a constitutional problem of India:

> *A foreigner is a foreigner; a foreigner shall not be judged by the language he speaks or by the religion he follows.* Communal considerations (either religious or linguistic) cannot be taken into account while determining the citizenship of a person; *the secular character of the Indian Constitution does not allow that.* (Emphasis in original; AASU and AAGSP 1980: 6)

Consequently, when they emphasized the "threat" caused by the large influx of foreigners, they were careful not to narrate it in terms of cultural, religious, or linguistic identity, but in the context of national security. To reinforce their argument, the AASU pointed to the Chinese aggression (Indo–China war) in 1962 and alleged that the Pakistan-(Bangladesh)-based immigrants had exhibited tacit support to the aggressors. In their words:

> While the indigenous population of Assam and NE [North East] region was preparing for whatever meager resistance they could offer to the Chinese invaders, *the flag of Pakistan was openly flown in many places of Assam by the illegal foreigners and their leaders, who were busy making preparations for welcoming the Chinese.* (Emphasis in original; AASU 1980b: 5)

This, however, does not mean that cultural, religious, or linguistic identities had lost their significance in contemporary Assamese society. While the AASU leaders were careful to avoid couching their claims in a communal tone, some of the organizations that supported the movement were less concerned about the matter and expressed their concern about the threat to the Assamese cultural identity posed by the influx of foreigners. For example, in a pamphlet issued by the Gauhati University Teachers' Association (GUTA), it was stated:

> Since the immigrants from Bangladesh (and former East Pakistan) were largely Muslims, the abnormal rise in the Muslim population in some of these districts (where the rise of population is high) is another clear indication of the fact that the growth rate was unnatural and the result of large-scale migration. (GUTA 1980: 3)

and

> The immigrants, though belong to two different religious groups, they come from same linguistic clan.... Another important, but significant feature of these immigrants is that for all practical purposes and even for trifle politico-social gains, these two diverge [*sic*] religious groups of immigrants combine on grounds of linguistic affinity at opportune time to create regional tension and bitterness. (GUTA 1980: 34)

It should be noted here that the GUTA was one of the organizations that closely sympathized with the AASU, and in fact, some of its members were in the frontline of the movement.

There are several implications that could be inferred from the statements made by the student leaders. First of all, there is a clear connection between the language movements of the 1960s and 1970s, and the antiforeigner movement, in terms of the leadership and its direction towards the preservation of Assamese identity. However, we can also see that there was a major change in the strategy adopted by the leaders of the movements. In the latter movement, the issue of language was kept out, and the students staked their claims primarily on the basis of population statistics and constitutional rights. In this sense, the AASU was making a serious bid to present a secular and constitutionally legitimate claim.

At the same time, as shown in the GUTA's pamphlets, there were also people who defined the problem in the context of language and on religious grounds. Here we can see the influence of past events on the antiforeigner movement in Assam. For many people who have experienced the language crisis and disturbances in the 1960s and 1970s, the newly-framed anti-foreigner movement was simply a continuation of the same struggle.

Comparing the linguistic movements and the antiforeigner movement, in the case of the former, Bengali-speaking people, especially Bengali Hindus, were tagged as the "Other." At the time of the antiforeigner movement, however, the category "Other" shifted from the cultural category "Bengali Hindus" to the political category "foreigners." This way, in their official demands, the movement leaders tried to legitimize the claim by pointing out the fact that there was a large-scale influx of population into Assam. Based on the abnormal increase of the population in Assam, the movement leaders tried to emphasize the gravity of the problem. At the same time, in order to avoid the communal tone in their official claims, they did not target any linguistic or religious groups.

Successful Mass Mobilization: "Peasant Nationalism" or "Gentry Nationalism"?

One particular character of the antiforeigner movement was that the leaders were successful in encouraging the participation of the masses. It should be noted that the linguistic movement was basically a middle-class movement. The demand for Assamese as the official language of the state was raised by the Asam Sahitya Sabha, the association of literary organizations and comprising the Assamese-speaking middle class. Moreover, the movement on the medium of instruction in the Gauhati University was led by student organizations. The linguistic issue was not only cultural but also related to employment issues, but it was only limited to jobs in the state administration. Therefore, it was primarily a concern of the educated classes. It was the same in the case of the movement on the medium of instruction in the universities; the masses or the rural peasants were indifferent to the matter.

Contrary to the language movements, the leaders of the antiforeigner movement were successful in mobilizing the masses. For example, in a satyagraha in November 1979, nearly 700,000 in the city of Guwahati and an estimated two million people in the state as a whole courted arrest. In the oil blockade in Duliajan, as many as 12,000 people participated in picketing. The blockade continued from December 27, 1979, to January 18, 1980, until the state administration used the police force to disperse them. Commenting on this situation, Hiren Gohain wrote, "The agitation over the presence of so-called 'foreign nationals' has grown into a massive movement, bringing out into the streets hundreds of thousands of ordinary men and women" (Gohain 1980a: 418).

There are two opposite views on the success of the mass mobilization. Many people in Assam interpreted it as a success of the movement leaders to represent the interest of the masses, including the rural peasants and the indigenous tribal groups. However, some people who opposed the movement, particularly the Marxists, insisted that the peasants and the indigenous peoples were utilized by the Assamese upper class to secure their own interest. For example, Hiren Gohain was of the view that it was the Assamese ruling elite who used the "cudgel of chauvinism" and beat the non-Assamese working class by inspiring the Assamese peasantry with a dream of refurbished "national" glory (Gohain 1980a: 420).

Moreover, Amalendu Guha argued that the current antiforeigner movement was "gentry nationalism" and not "peasant nationalism," in his long paper published in the *Economic and Political Weekly* (Guha 1980: 1705–9). Refuting the claim, Udayon Misra asserted that earlier Guha himself had acknowledged the fact that the clash of interests involved both the peasants and indigenous peoples. To quote:

> That the clash of interests was not confined to the Asamiya rich peasantry and the immigrants but also involved the urban middle class and the peasant masses is amply substantiated by Guha himself. "If the immigration continued unrestrained, would not the Assamese be turned into a linguistic minority in their own homeland—the Brahmaputra valley? This was the question which plagued the mind of not only its urban middle classes, but also the peasant masses." (Misra 1981: 291 quoting Guha 1977: 205–6)

On this point, Guha replied that the peasants were "misguided" by the rural gentry:

> If the force of nationalism behind the current anti-foreigner agitation is "gentry nationalism," how to explain the involvement of the peasantry, including those of tribal origin? We have already partially answered this. It may be added that acute economic stagnation, with the growing problems of indebtedness, landlessness and unemployment, is at the root of the general discontent. Peasants' discontent and their desire for increased autonomy has been exploited by vested interest and given a chauvinist twist. Ignorant, conservative and backward peasants have been misguided by the rural gentry. Instead of uniting the toilers of all communities, linguistic and religious, in a common anti-feudal, anti-monopoly struggle the movement has divided them on the basis of communalism and divisive slogans. (Guha 1981: 782)

This point is fundamental in understanding the character of the antiforeigner movement and the violence that broke out during the movement. The attackers of the violence were the indigenous groups and the Hindus of lower strata who are largely peasants. Whether the movement leaders could address the issues of the rural peasants and were successful in representing their interests is relevant to the discussion in the latter chapters of this book, especially where we examine the character of the Nellie massacre through the narratives of the attackers and the victims.

Loss of Land and Alienation of Tribes

One of the reasons for the success of the mobilization of the masses in the movement was that there was a demand for the deportation of foreigners, which was related to the issue of land, a major concern of the peasants including the indigenous tribal groups. At the time of the movement, the Muslims of East Bengal origins were numerically the biggest group perceived as illegal "foreigners." They were mainly peasants who held vast tracts of land in the lower and middle parts of Assam. If the movement would be successful and the demand for the deportation of the foreigners fulfilled, the land they owned would be abandoned. Thus, the major demand of the antiforeigner movement was related to the issue of land, which drew the attention of the rural peasants. In fact, there were peasants who were told by the movement leaders that the land of the "foreigners" would be given to them if they joined the movement.

This was especially a crucial issue for the indigenous tribal groups in the plains areas of Assam, such as the Bodos and the Tiwas. The plains indigenous communities in Assam once had a vast tract of land, but now had lost most of their traditional land. Many parts of the land were settled by the Muslims of Bengal origin. After India's independence, the tribal belts and blocks were created by government order to reserve the land for the "tribes" and prohibit non-tribal peoples to acquire the land in the tribal area. However, in many of the tribal belts and blocks, the system failed to function and the tribes gradually lost their land to the immigrants. The AASU and the AAGSP seized the issue and drew public attention to the problem of alienation of the indigenous communities from land. It was perhaps for the first time that the mainstream Assamese had seriously taken note of the matter. In the pamphlet issued in 1983, the AASU summed up the problem as follows:

> The problem has badly hit the tribal population. All the 37 Blocks and Belts reserved for the tribal people are on the verge of extinction. Pressure on economy has reduced the sizes of the reserved tribal blocks. Forest resources are fast disappearing due to indiscriminate felling of trees and occupation of the area by the foreign nationals. (AASU 1983a: 22)

It is true that the Muslims of Bengal origin were regarded as a main competing group who took away most of the land once owned by the tribes and other local communities. The growing number of the Muslim population in rural areas and the expansion of their settlements led many people to believe that Muslims were the ones who grabbed the lands from indigenous tribal groups.

Although such cases did exist, the image of "land-hungry Muslims" and their aggressiveness was largely exaggerated. For example, G. C. Sharma Thakur pointed out that most tribes lost their land due to their indebtedness to *mahajans*, the local moneylenders. He stated, "[t]he land hungry village tribal as well as non-tribal *mahajans* are keeping the poverty stricken tribals under their clutch for generations" (Sharma Thakur 1986: 101).

Indeed, the focus on the issue of land alienation of indigenous peoples by the movement leaders may be the main reason why the indigenous tribal groups supported, or at least sympathized with, the movement. For example, at that time the All Bodo Students' Union did not join the movement, but they were sympathetic to the cause of the movement. In areas where the indigenous groups did not have their own leadership, that is, Nagaon District, the AASU had a support among the plains indigenous people such as the Tiwas.

At the same time, the movement leaders made a controversial demand for deporting the foreigners from government-reserved land. They alleged that many foreigners had illegally occupied the government-reserved forests and emphasized the need for the eviction of the illegal encroachers. Given that many indigenous people also settled in the government forest along with the immigrants, the demand invited the opposition of a section of the indigenous groups in plains. The case was especially serious in the Gohpur area, where the Bodos and the Assamese people had a long-standing conflict over government land. In Gohpur reserved forest, the Bodo peasants had been settling there and cutting the forest. The government officials evicted them with the help of the non-tribal Assamese, and later allotted the same lands to the latter. This led to the Gohpur incident in 1983, in which Assamese people were killed by the Bodos.

Moreover, in 1985, when the central government and the AASU came to an agreement, there was one clause (clause 10) regarding the government land, and the tribal belts and blocks in the Memorandum of Settlement (popularly known as the Assam Accord). I quote:

> It will be ensured that relevant laws for prevention of encroachment on government land and lands in tribal belts and blocks are strictly enforced. Unauthorised encroachers will be evicted under such laws. It will be ensured that relevant laws restricting acquisition of immovable properties by foreigners in Assam will be strictly enforced. (The Assam Accord 1985)

This clause invited ambivalent responses from the indigenous peoples. Although the protection of the tribal belts and blocks was welcomed by the plains tribes, the demand for eviction from government land had serious implications for many of the indigenous people who had illegally cut the forest and resided there.

Moreover, in another clause (clause 6), it was emphasized that the central government would take special measures for the protection of cultural, social, and linguistic identity of the Assamese people, and there was no mention of the indigenous culture or identity:

> Constitutional, legislative and administrative safeguards as may be appropriate will be provided to protect the cultural, social and linguistic identity and heritage of the Assamese people. (The Assam Accord 1985)

Thus, the AASU and the AAGSP were successful in mobilizing the plains indigenous communities in the first phase of the movement, but in the end, they failed to recognize their social, cultural, and economic needs. These are some of the testimonies to be noted when we consider the relationship between the indigenous groups and the movement leaders, and their representation of the interest of the rural masses.

It should be noted here that although the movement was successful in gaining mass support, there were some differences in the interests and concerns of the urban middle class and the rural peasants. For the middle-class people, the movement was concerned with their identity, political hegemony, and employment, whereas for the rural peasants, the main issue was their land and livelihood.

At the same time, it is important to note that it was for the first time after independence that the people in Assam experienced such a large-scale movement which involved rural peasants. By participating in the movement, the rural masses came to know the importance of the idea of nationality in relation to the issues which affected their lives, such as land alienation. It may be the first time too that they were introduced to the idea that the Muslim immigrants are *bideshi* (foreigners). The idea that they are the original inhabitants of the land and hence they have the right to own the land, whereas the immigrants are "foreigners" who have no legal or political rights and therefore should be evicted, must have had a great impact on the rural peasants and indigenous communities.

Subsequently, when the movement leaders did not meet the economic and political aspirations of the indigenous groups, the latter's disappointment became much deeper than before. As will be shown in later chapters, this constitutes one of the most important causes for the influential movements by the indigenous peoples today. Thus, the impact of the movement on the rural peasants has multiple dimensions. It is prudent and imperative to pay attention to the peasants' own interests and their subjective activity when considering the issue of "mass participation" in the movement.

Nativist Movement and Rise of Regionalism

What made it possible for the movement leaders to mobilize mass participation in the late 1970s and 1980s? In Assam, antipathy against immigrants was often used by the movement leaders and political parties to mobilize support. Myron Weiner analyzed the linguistic movements in Assam and called it one of the nativist movements seen in other parts of India and postcolonial states. Such anti-immigrant movements can be seen in other states and countries where large-scale immigration took place during the colonial period.

In the 1970s and 1980s, this turned into regionalism movements in which the regional parties or organizations sought to negotiate power with the GOI. These moves were triggered by a split in the Congress party and

the formation of the Janata-led government in 1977. This led to the formation of regional parties in Assam and their alliance with the Janata party.

The AASU's antiforeigner movement started in such a political context
and became a force to challenge Congress rule in the state. Till then, the
Assamese Hindus and the Muslims of Bengal origin had supported the
Congress. After the movement started, most of the Assamese Hindus supported the AASU and asked for the deportation of "foreigners." The Congress
government tried to protect the largest vote bank, the Muslims, and did not
take up the demand to deport the foreigners who had crossed the border
after 1951. Faced with such political change, the movement started to target
the Muslims as "foreigners."

These political moves are important in understanding why the Muslims,
whose descendants came to Assam in the colonial period, became the target
of the attack during the antiforeigner movement. Let us look more closely
at the analyses of the nativist movement and political change in Assam at
this time in order to gain a better theoretical understanding.

"Sons of the Soil": Analysis of Nativist Movement by Myron Weiner

In the arguments that follow, I introduce Myron Weiner's analysis of the
structure of the Assamese society and economy on the nativist movement.
The scholar in question, an American political scientist, argues this point
by analyzing both the linguistic and antiforeigner movements in Assam.
He describes the linguistic movements as one of the nativist movements in
India in his book *Sons of the Soil*, which was published in 1978 just before
the movement started.

He conducted a comparative analysis of nativist movements in India and
called them movements by the "sons of the soil." He found close similarity
with the movements that occurred in postcolonial states such as Malaysia,
Uganda, and Indonesia, where large-scale immigration had taken place during
the colonial period. He surveyed the social stratification of each immigrant
group, and concluded that competition between the emerging middle class
of the "sons of the soil" and the "middle-man minority" caused ethnic tension in these areas (Weiner 1978).

Weiner referred to theories of ethnic conflict, such as the "dual labor market" of Michael Hechter and the "ethnic division of labor" or "middleman minority" of Edna Bonacich. He listed three major conditions under which competition among communities takes place. First, the ethnic division of labor between migrants (and their descendants) and non-migrants parallels class relationships that ordinarily have a high conflict potential. Second, the local population seeks access to occupations that they previously did not seek or from which they were once excluded. Weiner argued that when the local population produces its own educated class, which aspires to move into jobs held by the migrants, then middle-class nativist movements tend to happen. Third, a change in the power structure stimulates competition by giving one group the political resources for modifying or transforming the ethnic division of labor (Weiner 1978: 7–8).

He cited examples of countries such as Malaysia, Burma, and Uganda as well as provincial states like Assam and Maharashtra in India to support his argument. In most areas, large-scale immigration had taken place during the colonial period. In the case of Assam, large groups of poverty-stricken indigenous people had been imported from Orissa, Bihar, and Bengal as tea-plantation laborers by the colonial power. There were educated Bengalis who had been brought in to perform administrative jobs. The Muslim peasants of East Bengal had been lured and traded in to Assam for cultivation and consequently helped to increase state revenue. The Marwaris had been engaged in trade and had played an important role in opening Assam to the economic system of north India.

In short, immigrants had played an important role when Assam was assimilated into the modern, colonial, economic, industrial, and political systems. As a result, the employment in the modern sectors that came up with colonization was dominated by the immigrants. Viewed thus, so to say, it would not be wrong to assert that only by introducing large-scale immigration that the colonization of Assam was enabled.

Among the immigrants, the Marwaris and the middle-class Bengalis (mostly Hindus) were socially and economically successful. They were the main competitors of the emerging Assamese middle class, and these groups were the main targets of riots during the 1960s and the 1970s. They were the ones who did not accept Assamese as their mother tongue or medium of instruction, and hence became targets in the linguistic movement.

The Breakdown in the Assamese–Bengali-Muslim Coalition: Demographic and Political Approach

In 1983, soon after violence broke out during the State Legislative Assembly election in Assam, Myron Weiner wrote an article titled "The Political Demography of Assam's Anti-Immigrant Movement." In this paper, Weiner highlighted the change in the objective of the Assamese movement.

First, he pointed out that from the time of independence until 1977, there had been an "unspoken coalition" between the Assamese and the Muslims of Bengal origin. The Muslims of Bengal origin had even gone to the extent of declaring to census enumerators that Assamese was their native tongue, and had voted for the Assamese-dominated Congress party. The reason for this behavior, Weiner argued, was that the Muslims of Bengali origin feared that they could be driven out from the country. Thus, he stated,

> In an effort to dissuade the Assamese from taking these steps, Bengali Muslims sided with the Assamese on issues that mattered to them, by declaring their mother tongue as Assamese, accepting the establishment of primary and secondary schools in Assamese, supporting the government against Bengali Hindus on the controversial issue of an official language for the state and for the university, and casting their votes for Congress. (Weiner 1983: 285)

Weiner saw 1977 as the turning point in Assamese–Bengali relations. The Assamese turned against the Muslims of Bengal origin for both demographic and political reasons. There had been an illegal influx of Bengal Muslims from erstwhile East Pakistan, now Bangladesh. In the 1971 census, it had been reported that there was a great increase in the Muslim population. Moreover, the civil war in East Pakistan in 1971 and the 1972 war between India and Pakistan had again caused the population to increase, and Weiner concluded that there had been immigration of 1.8 million into Assam from 1971 to 1981. This had led to renewed fear among the Assamese that they would become a minority in their own state.

Moreover, in 1977, the Congress Party had split into two factions in Assam, as elsewhere in India. As a consequence, in the March 1978 election, for the first time after the country's partition, the Congress party had failed to win a majority in the state assembly. This split within the Congress had ended the postindependence coalition of the Assamese Hindus and the Bengali Muslims. Some Bengali Muslims had shifted their support to other parties such as the Communist Party of India (CPI) and the Communist Party of India (Marxist) (CPI[M]). The two parties (the CPI and CPI[M]) had increased their seats in the election and combined together, they held 16 seats. Many Assamese, however, regarded the communist parties as synonymous with the Bengalis because of the dominant procommunist vote in both West Bengal and Tripura.

After pointing out the political change, Weiner concluded thus:

> The end of the alliance between Assamese Hindus and Bengali Muslims thus resulted from a series of events: the continued influx of Bengali Muslims from Bangladesh, the split in the Congress Party, the shift of some Bengali Muslims to the leftist parties, the opposition of Assamese Hindu middle-class landowners to the demands of their Muslim tenants, and the efforts by political parties and groups opposed to the leftist parties and the Congress (I) to reduce the size of the Bengali electorate. (Weiner 1983: 289)

In this way, the target of the movement was largely decided by political motives rather than the social change at the time. In electoral politics, the number of votes is important and in this sense, middle-class Bengalis (mostly Hindus) were not numerically strong. Rather, the Muslim peasants of Bengal origin, who were the solid vote bank of the Congress, emerged as a target.

It was both urban youth and rural peasants who most actively involved in the boycott and violence during the State Legislative Assembly election in 1983. The issues of unemployment among urban middle-class youth and the land issues among rural peasants were the factors which led them to participate in the boycott and violence. The movement leaders, however, were mainly urban middle-class youth and when the movement came to an end, the indigenous people's aspirations and demands were not incorporated in the Assam Accord as we have seen earlier. In this sense, the leftists' critique that the movement leaders were only exploiting the discontent and the aspirations of tribes and peasants was right. The movement leaders might have been sincere in raising the issues of land alienation among the indigenous peoples and peasants in the beginning, but the middle-class leadership principally failed to reflect the demand in the Assam Accord and in the policies after they came to power.

Who Are the Foreigners? The Fear of Minoritization

For people who live outside Assam, it has been a puzzle why the movement demanding deportation of foreigners turned against almost all the outsiders, particularly the Muslims of Bengal origin. The majority of the so-called outsiders were descendants of the immigrants who had migrated to Assam in the colonial period. In order to understand this point, it is necessary to know that there was an apprehension among the Assamese-speaking people that they were being minoritized in their own state. In Assam, the Muslims constituted 25 percent of the population at the time of independence, and their percentage was growing. Combined with other immigrants, such as the tea-garden tribes who have their origins in the Chotanagpur plateau, the Nepalis and other Hindi-speaking population, the descendants of immigrants who migrated to Assam during the colonial period comprised more than 40 percent of the population of Assam.

Student leaders also exaggerated the figure and attributed all the population increase to "foreign influx." Some scholars, especially those who have their origins in Bengal, refuted and the debate arose as to who were the foreigners and how many of them were there in Assam after the AASU launched the movement. To gain a better understanding of the situation at the time, let us scrutinize some of the arguments on the estimation of number of foreigners and on the cutoff year. What is striking in the arguments is that there did not exist a consensus on the definition of "foreigners" and hence there was difficulty in reaching the agreement on the number of foreigners, and that some arguments arose on the issue of the cutoff year. Such disagreement on the definition and the cutoff year not only arose between the GOI and the student leaders, but also with the Bengali middle-class people who saw the movement as mostly against Bengalis.

Politics of Counting "Foreigners"

With the influx of foreigners, from across the border, that accompanied the liberation of Bangladesh, the threat perception assumed a new reality and hence the number of foreigners was one of the main foci of the arguments by the movement leaders. However, there were several difficulties in estimating the number of foreigners, as there were no official statistics on the "illegal immigrants," contributing to the polarization in the debate not only on the existence of the foreigners but also on the legitimacy of the movement. Many scholars pointed out that there had been an abnormal population increase in Assam in the decades following independence. At the time of the antiforeigner movement various arguments were advanced on the cause of the increase. I will examine the statistics from the Indian census and highlight some of the key arguments on the number of foreigners.

The census statistics show that the total population of Assam was 8,029,000 in 1951, 10,837,000 in 1961, and 14,625,000 in 1971. The growth rate of 1951 to 1961 was 34.97 percent and that of 1961 to 1971 was 34.95 percent. If we compare the growth rate with the all-India averages, which were 21.64 percent and 24.80 percent respectively, the percentage is much larger in Assam (Table 3.1).

Table 3.1
The Growth of Population in Assam

Year	Population	Increase	Increase in Assam (%)	Increase in India (%)
1901	3,290,000	–	–	–
1911	3,849,000	559,000	16.99	5.73
1921	4,637,000	788,000	20.47	0.30
1931	5,561,000	924,000	19.92	11.00
1941	6,694,000	1,133,000	20.37	14.23
1951	8,029,000	1,335,000	19.94	13.31
1961	10,837,000	2,808,000	34.97	21.64
1971	14,625,000	3,788,000	34.95	24.80
1981	19,100,000	4,475,000	30.60	20.60

Sources: Census of India 1971, Dass 1980: 851.
Note: Figures of 1981 are estimates, as census was not taken in 1981 in Assam.

In 1981, the census was not taken in Assam as the movement leaders were opposed to its enumeration. There are, however, several estimates available on the population of Assam during the period. For example, Myron Weiner cited it as 19.9 million (Weiner 1983: 286, 291). Susanta Krishna Dass calculated the population on the basis of the 1979 figures and estimated it to be 19.1 million. Even if we take the smaller of the two numbers, the population growth rate of 1971–1981 would be 30.60 percent (Dass 1980: 851). Based on census statistics, the AASU leaders calculated that there were at least 4.5 million foreigners in Assam. In a pamphlet circulated by the Union, it stated:

> A conservative estimate of the infiltrators' number is over 45 lakh of whom over 15 lakh have entered their names in the electoral rolls, thus causing serious demographic imbalances.... National Average for population increase per decade—22%. Adding a 22% increase for the decade, the population of Assam which was 10,837,329 in 1961 should have been 11,950,149 in 1971 but the actual figure recorded in 1971 is 14,625,152!.... The excess population in Assam over the national figures comes to 2,675,003 (26 lakh). Thus in 1971 itself Assam had an abnormal growth to the tune of 26 lakh! Projected to 1980, the increase in excess of normal limits shall be of order of 51,647,740 (51 lakh!). (AASU 1980a: 2–3)

The AASU leaders attributed most of the excess increase in population to the influx of immigrants from foreign countries. As they did not consider migration from other parts of India and the natural growth rate, their estimate of 4.5 million could be an exaggeration. However, it is a fact that at the time, there was an abnormal increase in the population of Assam and the movement leaders had reason to believe that they were engulfed by immigrants.

However, there were several arguments to counter the figure on the foreigners' influx cited by the movement leaders. As the abnormal population growth in Assam was clear, critics pointed out other causes, such as the increase in the natural growth rate or the influx of refugees (not "foreigners"), for the increasing population or the fact that the immigrants had assimilated to the Assamese society and so they could not be seen as a threat in Assam.

Susanta Krishna Dass, a demographer of Bengali origin, pointed out three causes for the high rate of increase in Assam's population from 1951. They were: (1) the natural rate of increase; (2) influx of Hindu refugees from East Pakistan; and (3) heavier migration of Indians from the rest of the country. Dass examined census data and concluded that the apprehensions about "infiltration" of the Bangladeshi or East Pakistani Muslims into Assam appeared not to be supported by empirical facts (Dass 1980: 850–59).

Amalendu Guha, a historian and another Bengali scholar, argued that the number of foreigners would be no more than 1.3 million. He stated:

It appears, as per our quick estimates, that the number of post-1951 settlers with questionable citizenship status would in no case exceed 13 lakh by any measure and that the number of persons born in Pakistan (including Bangladesh) and enumerated in Assam shows a declining trend over the period 1951–1971. (Guha 1980: 1710)

Moreover, Guha confidently asserted that the Muslims of Bengal origin had already assimilated or on their way to assimilation.

At the time of the movement, these criticisms on exaggerating the numbers often came from Bengali scholars. However, what is a matter of concern is that rather than encouraging a serious debate on the foreigners' issue, the arguments advanced by the critics were taken as another attempt of the Bengalis to protect migrants of common origin. The issue of division between the Assamese and the Bengalis is discussed in later chapters, but it should be noted that there is a serious disagreement between the two communities, and it starts from basic points such as the number of immigrants and the definition of foreigners.

Recently, there has been a summary report, *Migration to Assam: 1951–1991*, produced by the Omeo Kumar Das Institute of Social Change and Development. The aim of the report was to provide a scientific explanation for the growth of population in Assam from 1951 to 1991. The report was based on census population data and Sample Registration System estimates of fertility and mortality rates. It estimated the total international migrants between the years 1951 to 1991 to be 1,983,755 persons, and among them, the number of illegal foreign migrants to be nearly 1.3 million (Goswami et al. 2002). If we accept the estimation of the report, then the number of illegal migrants was much less than that claimed by the AASU, but still it was a considerable number.

The Issue of Cutoff Year: 1951 or 1971?

Another factor that added to the confusion over the size and issue of foreign infiltration was the disagreement on the cutoff year between the AASU leaders and the central government. The AASU demanded that 1951 should be the cutoff year for the identification and deportation of foreign nationals, while the central government did not accept the demand and instead suggested 1971 as the alternative.

Based on the Constitution and other acts such as The Citizenship Act, 1955, and The Immigrant (Expulsions from Assam) Act, 1950, the AASU argued:

> Under Article 5 of the Constitution of India no person who did not have domicile in India at the commencement of the Constitution could be a citizen of India. Thus under this provision all persons who came to India after January 26, 1950, could not be citizens of India. But Article 11 gave power to the Parliament to make law for the acquisition of citizenship by birth, descent, registration or naturalization. Thus a person entering India after January 26, 1950, and did not acquire citizenship under any of the provisions of the Indian Citizenship Act, 1955, remained a foreigner. (AASU 1980a: 12)

Further, the AASU proposed that the National Register of Citizens for Assam, a document prepared by census enumerators from the census slips of 1951, should be employed as the basis for ascertaining the identity of migrants who came after 1951 (AASU 1980a: 12–13).

On the other hand, the GOI proposed March 1971 as the cutoff date, on the ground that Bangladesh gained independence that year. The Congress party, the ruling party at the center at the time, had depended for much of its support in Assam on the Bengali Muslims, and they were reluctant to accept the demand to deport them. As the government was ready to accept other major demands, it was because of this issue that a stalemate between the AASU and the government ensued.

The disagreements over the cutoff year were not resolved until the end of the movement in 1985, when the AASU accepted the Assam Accord which stated the cutoff year as 1971. Thus, during the movement, there was no consensus between the GOI and the movement leaders on the definition of foreigners.

Moreover, there was some ambiguity about the status of Hindu immigrants who had crossed the border into India after 1950. The Immigrant (Expulsions from Assam) Act, 1950 implicitly distinguished the Hindu refugees and the Muslim illegal aliens. Although the law was repealed in 1957, it has been revealed that there was a secret administrative order from the GOI in 1965 which had instructed that East Pakistani minorities, that is the Hindus settled in India for more than six months, could be granted citizenship by a district magistrate following some easy procedure (Baruah 1999: 119).

Thus, there has been a belief among the Bengali Hindus who came to India from Pakistan that they should be treated as refugees and given citizenship. However, the Assamese people did not accept this view, and the movement leaders defined the foreigners irrespective of their religion.

In this way, there was a major difference between the center's point of view and the movement leaders' claims. The central government, who regarded the illegal immigrants as their vote bank, did not accept the movement leaders' demands that they be deported. Neighboring Bengali media and intellectuals reacted emotionally and did not even admit the existing problems.

Amidst these circumstances, the movement leaders who had gained overall support by pointing out the fear of minoritization continued to make a claim for deportation. In this way, the political solution to the problem could not be reached even after three years of the movement, and it led to disastrous clashes between the communities during the 1983 election.

4

Election Boycott and the Nellie Incident

In January 1983, the Congress-led Government of India (GOI) announced its decision to hold an election for the 126-member Assam State Legislative Assembly and 12 Lok Sabha constituencies, vacant since the 1980 poll, without revising the electoral rolls. The movement leaders, who openly claimed opposition to the election whereby the names of foreigners would not be deleted from the electoral rolls, decided to boycott the election. This led to the mobilization of the masses again, and the All Assam Students' Union (AASU) workers and supporters tried their best to prevent the election from taking place in Assam.

The GOI arrested top AASU leaders, including Prafulla Kumar Mahanta and Bhrigu Phukan, on January 6, 1983, at the airport, as they were on their way back from failed talks with the central government on this issue. Almost at the same time, the GOI announced that the election would be held on February 14, 17, and 20. The Government of Assam ordered the *Assam Tribune* and the *Dainik Asom*, two prominent local daily newspapers that supported and led the movement, to restrain from publishing any matter relating to the current agitation, thus showing a strong tendency towards press censorship.

The leadership was replaced by second-rank leaders. Nagen Sarma and Nurul Hussain temporarily took over the roles of president and general secretary respectively. In cooperation with the All Guwahati Students' Union and the All Kamrup District Students' Union, they organized the antielection campaign. The movement leaders called the boycott "Assam's last struggle for survival" and campaigned widely. They used all means to stop the election administration, including burning bridges and blocking roads to stop candidates from filing nominations, and preventing access to polling booths. Some of them even kidnapped family members and relatives of the candidates to cancel their nominations. According to the Tewary Commission, which was appointed as the official commission of enquiry on the election disturbances in July 1983, there were: 545 attacks on roads and bridges from January to March; 140 kidnappings; 193 attacks on election staff and candidates, their relatives, or political workers; 274 bomb explosions or recoveries of explosives; and so on (Tewary Commission Report 1984: 424–25). As a result, only 630 candidates filed nominations, compared to 1,049 at the time of the 1978 assembly elections. The AASU and the All Assam Gana Sangram Parishad (AAGSP) were successful in ensuring that the opposition parties, the two Lok Dal factions—the Bharatiya Janata Party and the Janata Party—boycotted the election. The Congress, the six-party Left Democratic Alliance (the Congress [S], the Communist Party of India [Marxist], the Communist Party of India, the Revolutionary Communist Party of India, the Socialist Unity Centre of India, and the Revolutionary Socialist Party), and a local Assamese party among indigenous tribal groups, called the Plains Tribal Council of Assam (PTCA), decided to contest the election.

The boycott was supported not only by a handful of extremists or radical student activists, but also by the majority of the local Assamese citizens. The AASU and the AAGSP called upon government officials to boycott their offices on January 17 and for a 35-hour *bandh* (general strike) from the following morning. This resulted in large numbers of employees staying away from work in spite of the state administration's threat to come down heavily with the Essential Services Maintenance Act (Kalbag 1983: 14–15).

As a result, the government had to bring about 8,000 officers, probationers and other workers from other states of the country for polling duty (Shourie 1983: 32). Moreover, about 55 battalions of the Central Reserve Police Force (CRPF), 36 battalions of the Haryana Armed Police, the Rajasthan Armed Constabulary, and the Provincial Armed Constabulary of Uttar Pradesh were brought into the state in order to conduct the elections. Along with the Assam Police's Armed sections, the Border Security Force, and the Home Guards, a conservative estimate would reach a total of 150,000 armed men in uniform in place to enforce law and order—one army man for every 57 voters—turning Assam into a military battleground rather than a political state suitable to democratically elect political representatives (Kalbag 1983: 15). As a result, the question was not who would win but whether the election would be held democratically at all.

The violence became visible at the end of January when the nominations came to an end. The AASU and the AAGSP announced their self-styled "janata curfew" (people's curfew), "janata bandh," and even "janata arrest" of violators of the boycott, as well as citywide blackouts as a means of "satyagraha"[1] and to prevent election preparations and the filing of nominations. To counter the agitation, overall 290 police firing and *lathi* charge[2] were reported (Tewary Commission Report 1984: 427–55).

Amidst such tense circumstances, large-scale group clashes began to take place from February 11, 1983. The first large-scale clashes were reported from Gohpur in Darrang District on the northern bank of the Brahmaputra River. Then news came that a mass killing had occurred in a place called Nellie in Nagaon District. On February 18, 1983, about 1,600 to 2,000 Muslims of East Bengal origin were killed in several villages around Nellie. The attackers were mainly the Tiwas, the indigenous people whose kingdom was in this area, as well as other local residents, including the Kochs and the Hiras, who are Hindus of lower status. It has been said that several thousands of local residents were involved in the attack.

In the state of Assam, such a so-called riot has been rare. Apart from the disturbance that took place after 1951, the area is seen as relatively free from "Hindu–Muslim communal riots." Although the Northeast region has seen armed struggles in Nagaland and Mizoram, such a type of collective violence, or so-called riots, in which one group of civilians attacks another group, is rarely seen.

It should also be noted that the Nellie incident was one of the largest acts of collective violence that took place in India's rural areas since the Partition violence. In India, more than 90 percent of collective violence takes place in urban areas. There have been cases of large-scale riots such as the Bhagalpur riot in Bihar, but in this case, the violence started in the town and spread to rural areas. On the contrary, during the election disturbance in Assam in 1983, most killings took place in rural areas such as Nellie, Gohpur, and Chaolkhowa.

The Antiforeigner Movement and the Violence

The Muslims of immigrant origin were often harassed as "foreigners" and became the target of violence in the early phase of the antiforeigner movement. In the beginning of the movement, many Muslim students of East Bengal origin supported and joined the movement. However, as soon as their community was targeted, they turned against it or slowly withdrew their support, especially after the violence against the community in North Kamrup in

1980. In January, there was a series of incidents in North Kamrup, triggered by the death of a high-school student who had worked as a member of the AASU. He was killed in a village inhabited by the Muslims of East Bengal origin. His death resulted in a series of attacks and counterattacks between Assamese and immigrant villages, and a curfew was imposed in the area. Many of the victims were immigrants, and it was alleged that the army had committed atrocities on the Assamese villagers during the curfew, under the auspices of carrying out an investigation. This was the first large-scale group clash reported during the movement. Apart from the incidents in North Kamrup, the first half of 1980 saw disturbances such as police firing in upper Assam and a countermovement by the All Assam Minority Students' Union (AAMSU) in Goalpara.

The AASU did not strongly condemn the violence perpetrated against the Muslims of immigrant origin. Rather, they had a confrontation with the AAMSU and created an atmosphere of ostracizing people who were against the movement. They used slogans such as, "If you are an Assamese, you should join the movement," suggesting that people who did not join the movement were betraying the Assamese cause and subject to attack. In fact, at the time of the Nellie incident, there were allegations of low-ranking Assam state police officers collaborating with, or at least failing to stop, the attackers. A few of these cases were investigated and confirmed true by a government inquiry commission.

In the latter part of 1980, the central government became oppressive towards the movement. Mass support did not last long, and from 1981 to 1982, the movement stagnated. The violence during the election disturbance was of a scale that had never been seen in Assam's history, and was completely different from the violence that had occurred earlier during the antiforeigner movement. According to official records, from 1979 to December 1982, there were 272 murders, 1,404 assaults, 425 cases of arson, and 330 cases of explosion and recovery of explosives (DAVP 1983, cited in Narayan 2008: 22). However, during the election disturbance, the death toll reached 3,000 according to the official report (Tewary Commission Report 1984: 424–25). A journalist estimated that 7,000 people lost their lives during this period (Gupta 1984: 16).

The AASU's call for boycott triggered widespread violence. Some pointed out that since the moderate top leaders were arrested by the government, during the election, radical elements in the organization occupied the leadership. It is true that paramilitary wings such as the Jatiyatabadi Yuba Chatra

Parishad and the Swecha Sevak Bahini existed, and they also played a role in instigating violence (*India Today*, February 28, 1983). At the same time, the violence took place more in rural areas rather than the urban Guwahati, where the movement leaders were located. We need to examine what kind of local factors led to large-scale violence in remote areas such as Chaolkhowa, Gohpur, or even Nellie.

During this period, the Muslims of immigrant origin were the worst affected by the violence. Without the atmosphere and legitimacy provided to attack the Muslims, we would never be able to explain police negligence towards the violence. Rather than directly controlling the attack, the role of the movement leaders was more to set the agenda and define the important "Other" in the state. By defining them as "Bangladeshi," the movement and its ideology provided legitimacy to harass the Muslims and other minorities in the state. Such an ideology was shared by most sectors of the Assamese population, including government officers and police personnel. It led to situations where even if acts of violence were taking place against innocent minorities, their neighbors and police personnel did not dare stop them. In this way, the movement leaders provided the conditions making it possible to create a riot.

At the same time, the Muslims were not the only group targeted. The movement was interpreted in local contexts, and communities such as Nepalis, tea-garden laborers, Bengali Hindus, and sometimes even local Assamese people became the victims of violence. The fact that the Muslims of East Bengal origin were not the only victims of the violence shows that local politics also played an important role in the attacks.

The Nellie Incident

Nellie is situated 70 km east of Guwahati, the capital of Assam. It is situated on the highway that leads to Nagaon, the district headquarters of one of the oldest districts in Assam, and is about two hours away from Guwahati. Erstwhile Nagaon District, which included Nellie village until 1989, was generally agrarian, and villages around Nellie also produced paddy and jute. They were inhabited by Muslims of East Bengal origin, indigenous peoples (tribes) such as the Tiwas, and Assamese Hindus. In this locality, there were not many caste-Hindus, and most belonged to Scheduled Castes such as the Hiras and the Koibortas, or Other Backward Classes such as the Kochs. (The Kochs are said to have indigenous origins.)

In Nellie, *haat* (a weekly market) takes place every Monday. At an open place just in front of the national highway and adjacent to a school, people from neighboring villages come and sell their agricultural products and buy their daily necessities. During the *haat*, so-called hill Tiwas, who reside in the mountainous areas of neighboring Karbi Anglong District, travel from their home two kilometers away to buy and sell products.

There is a middle school and a high school in Nellie, as well as a market with a pharmacy, public call offices, grocery stores, and tailors on the highway. Men of influence or in middle-class occupations in this area tend to own houses on the highway around Nellie village. Caste-Hindus who need to settle in this area for their occupation also gather around this market. Villages of the Muslims, on the other hand, as well as of the Tiwas and others (Other Backward Classes and Scheduled Castes) are situated away from the highway, towards the Kopili River. The Nellie incident took place in the Muslim villages about 10 km north of Nellie village. For the reason that relief camps are set up in the middle school and the high school in the Nellie village, it is called the "Nellie massacre" even today. Most of the victims, however, belonged to ten villages in the northern part of Nellie, just south of Kopili River. These are mostly Muslim villages, but bounded by Tiwa and Koch villages in the south and the north.

Before British occupation, there was a Tiwa kingdom in Gobha, an area adjacent to the Nellie area. Thus, the area had a large Tiwa population as well as other plains tribes and Assamese Hindus of lower strata. After British colonization, however, in the early part of the 20th century, the colonial administration introduced an immigration policy by which large numbers of the Muslims from Eastern Bengal migrated. The present state of Assam was a scarcely populated area, and in order to increase income revenues, British colonial officers tried to settle immigrants in western and middle Assam. At that time, East Bengal was a congested area and landless peasants had a motivation to go to Assam to obtain land.

The northern part of Nagaon District, just south of the Brahmaputra River, was one of the first places where the Muslim immigrants settled. When the Muslim population increased due to fresh immigration and natural increase, they slowly started to settle in the southern part of the district. The villages targeted in the Nellie incident were in a grazing reserve that the neighboring villagers used for grazing cattle until the beginning of the 1940s.

The area is adjacent to the Kopili River and very prone to floods. This area was dereserved in order to settle immigrants during the Muslim League's regime, which facilitated the "Grow More Food" scheme.

The area now falls under the jurisdiction of the newly created Morigaon District. The district still has a mixed population where the Muslims are the majority in the north, and the indigenous peoples and the Assamese Hindus are majority in the south. Under these circumstances, in 1983, when the situation became tense between the immigrant community and the natives during the State Legislative Assembly election, the Tiwas and other local Hindus were targeted in the northern part and the Muslim peasants were targeted in the southern part.

Before the attack in Nellie, the entire Nagaon District was in turmoil due to the AASU's attempt to block access to polling stations in order to boycott the election. Group clashes took place between different ethnic, religious, and linguistic communities, such as the Assamese Hindus, the tribes, and the Muslims and Hindus of Bengal origin. In Nagaon, the Muslims were supporters of the Congress party, and before the incident, Congress leaders such as Indira Gandhi and Ghani Khan Choudhury visited minority pockets and made provocative speeches (Mehta Commission Report 1985: 47). Due to their immigrant origins, the Muslims had decided to vote for the Congress, also hoping that the new government would be able to put an end to the movement. The AASU, however, had its support base in indigenous tribal groups and other Hindus (mainly backward) in the area, and thus, the tension between the Muslims and the Tiwas increased.

According to a report by the Lalung [an old name for the Tiwas] Durbar submitted after the Nellie incident, the Tiwas were attacked by the Muslims in the area, north of Nellie. There was a report that several Tiwa children were killed and disposed of just before the Nellie incident. In the southern part, however, the Muslims, who were outnumbered by the Hindus, felt threatened, and had reported the possibility of an attack to the police several times before the incident. Some police officers visited the Muslim village and assured them of their safety but did not leave a patrol due to the lack of personnel.

On that fateful day, the attack began in the morning, starting in a village called Borbori, situated northeast of Nellie. After they finished the attack on Borbori, they crossed the national highway and started to attack the Muslim villages south of the Kopili. They encircled from the east, the south, and the north, and started to burn the houses. Hemendra Narayan, a journalist with the *Indian Express* at that time, witnessed the incident and reported:

In a systematic manner the houses of Muslim settlements at Demalgaon… were burnt.… As I rushed behind them, hundreds more out spaced me. Soon, one by one the houses on the Demalgaon were on fire. First, a bit of whitish smoke, then thick black smoke bellowed up. In half a minute, it was a red glare and within five minutes, the bare skeleton of the house remained. (*Indian Express*, February 19, 1983. Reproduced in Narayan 2008: 12)

After burning houses and leaving no place to hide, the attackers started to kill the Muslim villagers. People began to run towards the west, where the CRPF was located. Again, I quote from Narayan:

The immigrants fled to cross Demal Bil (rivulet) to be in Muladhari village..... As the houses were burnt, all the tribals assembled on the high bank. The immigrants could be seen assembled across the rivulet in Muladhari. Others from Alisingha, Silcherri and Baihati were already there. Arrows and stones were exchanged across the Bil. The shouts and screams reached a crescendo.… The situation took a turn when another group or tribals appeared from the eastern side of Muladhari.… Vastly outnumbered Muslims had no other choice but to run. But they were trapped. On one side was Demal River and further north another river Kopili. They ran to the west to the Bhutnimara village on the foothills. In a desperate dash for survival, the women and children could not keep pace with the men. One by one, they were hacked to death by hundreds of rampaging tribals. So they were first to be hacked with daos. Standing on the other bank of Demal I could count 22 women lying on the already harvested paddy fields. (*Indian Express*, February 19, 1983. Reproduced in Narayan 2008: 13)

People who could reach the CRPF camp were able to save their lives, but many women, children, and elderly people were sacrificed. Among the victims, 70 percent were women, 20 percent were elderly, and 10 percent were men (Mehta Commission Report 1985: 167).

Between three and half past three in the afternoon, only when the CRPF troops reached the site of the attack, did the attackers stop the killing and disperse. From the Tewary Commission Report, it was revealed that the report of the attack reached the Jagiroad Police Station much earlier. At about half past twelve, the report of the attack reached the police station, and if the police had taken necessary action, they could have prevented a large number of deaths. It has been also alleged that some local police joined in the attack. This will be discussed in the latter part of this chapter.

After the attack, the villagers who lost their houses stayed in refugee camps set up in Nellie. The government provided security personnel to guard the place, and within six months to one year, most survivors had returned to their villages.

About 688 cases were filed at the police station regarding the Nellie incident. Among them, the police submitted charge sheets in 310 cases. In 1985, however, when the movement leaders formed the Asom Gana Parishad and became the ruling party, all cases concerning the 1983 election were closed. Thus, nobody has been punished for this incident so far.

At that time, there were about 6,000 to 7,000 Muslims[3] residing in the area. The Mehta Commission Report states that in the incident, about 1,600 people lost their lives. Some people estimate that the death toll reached 2,000. Whatever the number is, it was an intensive killing that had never been seen before in Assam. Even today, if you visit the affected villages in the Nellie area, almost everybody says that they lost several members of their family in the incident.

Land as a Structural Cause for the Violence

Before analyzing the Nellie incident in detail, let us go through a few other incidents that took place during the election disturbance in 1983. As stated, group clashes took place not only between the natives and the Muslims of immigrant origin, but among almost all communities in Assam. Violence was seen in almost all the districts in the Assam valley, especially in the western and the middle areas of the state. Nagaon was one of the worst affected districts, and so was Darrang, the district situated to the north of the Brahmaputra River.

Another large-scale killing took place in Gohpur, one of the reserved forests in the district. From the 1970s onwards, the Bodos, another indigenous tribal group who had been displaced from western Assam, began to settle in the forest area. The Mehta Commission Report states that the Bodo people had migrated to the border areas of Nagaland and Assam, but on facing many troubles in the area, had again migrated to the north bank of the Brahmaputra River. There was a confrontation between caste-Hindu Assamese and Bodo people regarding the occupation of forestland before the incident (Mehta Commission Report 1985: 168).

Politically, the Bodos supported the PTCA, which aimed to carve out a separate state called "Udayachal" for different tribes in Assam. Regarding the antiforeigner movement, the different indigenous groups did not have a unified stance. Thus, in Nellie the Tiwas supported the movement, while in other areas, many indigenous student leaders joined the movement in the beginning but later turned against it. During the election period, the PTCA decided to contest the election and confronted the AASU, who were working to boycott the election. Thus, from the beginning of February, small-scale attacks on Assamese began, starting with the Bodos. It was followed by a large-scale attack in the Gohpur area, where more than 100 Assamese people lost their lives. It has been reported that ex–tea-garden laborers as well as Bengalis of immigrant origin too joined the attack (Mehta Commission Report 1985: 168–70).

A similar incident took place between the Muslims of immigrant origin and the Assamese in *char* (river island) areas of Darrang District. The Muslims of Bengali origin had occupied this area since migrating in the colonial period. The Assamese Hindus started to cultivate the *chapori*s (alluvial riverine land) near the char area, which led to confrontation between the two communities. During the election disturbance, the Muslims attacked the Assamese settlements and over 20 people were killed according to the Mehta Commission Report.

By looking at the Gohpur and Chaolkhowa incidents, as well as reports by both official and nonofficial inquiry commissions, we can point out some important factors regarding the disturbance during the 1983 election in Assam. First, it can be noted that the land dispute was one of the key factors behind the group clashes. It is worth noting that these attacks took place in forest and riverine areas where land ownership was not very clear. Regarding the Gohpur incident, it was near the reserved forest areas where the Bodo people started to reside in the 1970s. Officially the Bodo residents did not have land ownership and were, legally speaking, "encroachers." As for the Chaolkhowa incident, it took place in char areas where land ownership tends to be controversial since the boundaries in char and chapori areas change quite often due to the change in the course of the Brahmaputra River. If we consider that the Nellie area was also a grazing reserve till the 1940s, we can argue that land disputes tend to take place in areas where land ownership was not very clear till decades ago. Such reserves were first categorized as "wasteland" under British land systems as they were not cultivated. Although such land was not cultivated regularly, most of the land was utilized by original inhabitants in some way or the other. For example, some were utilized for grazing cattle, and others were *pam* lands, which were cultivated seasonally. The indigenous people undertook shifting cultivation even in the plain areas, of 10–15 years' cycle. These were community lands utilized by neighboring villagers but arbitrarily categorized as "wasteland" once the British colonizers found that the villagers could not afford to pay revenues annually.

It should also be noted that, when we examine the communities statewise, there was no fixed pattern in who the victims or the attackers were. The weaker sections of society suffered everywhere. This can be verified from both official and nonofficial inquiry commissions' reports. The Mehta Commission Report provides outlines of more than 70 group clashes. Among them, 37 took place between the immigrant Muslims and the Assamese; 27 between the immigrant Muslims and the Assamese tribals/Muslims; 2 between the Assamese tribals and the non-tribals; 8 between the Bengali Hindus and the Assamese; and 2 between the tea-garden tribes and the Assamese (Mehta Commission Report 1985: 145–76).

Group clashes were prevalent in the districts of the Brahmaputra valley. The total number of clashes was indeed not clear. It depends upon the way in which the various clashes are counted, as pointed out in the Tewary Commission Report. According to the latter's tolls, a total of 273 cases of group clashes were reported. Among these, 78 incidents took place in Darrang District, 52 in Nagaon, 48 in Goalpara, 28 in Sonitpur, and 26 in Kokrajhar. This shows the magnitude of the disturbance during the State Legislative Assembly election in 1983. There was a significant crisis in the situation of law and order at that time.

That land was an important factor in the attack partly explains the high toll of Muslim casualties, and also the high number of attackers in indigenous tribal areas. The Muslims of immigrant origin were mainly seen as the ones who grabbed land from local populations, especially the indigenous people. Thus, it is no wonder that many critics of the movement analyzed that primarily land issues had triggered the incident. However, the existence of land issues only explains part of the reason why there were attacks. As I have argued, immigration started in the early part of the twentieth century and, till then, land alienation was an important issue among the tribes in plains areas in lower and middle Assam. In order to explain the link between the violence and the land issue, we have to look at the kind of politics that played out during the incident in the particular area.

Relationship between the Movement Leaders and the Attackers in the Nellie Incident

The relationship between the movement leaders, the AASU and the AAGSP, and the local residents who participated in the attack is important in understanding the Nellie incident. However, so far there have been very few analyses based on fieldwork or empirical data on this issue. Some people, particularly those who were opposed to the antiforeigner movement have argued that the Nellie incident was instigated by the movement leaders. For example, Monirul Hussain stated:

> The role of the Lalungs who were involved in killings were peripheral like that of the hangman in capital punishment. The powerful forces from behind, systematically prepared the ground, gave the verdict for genocide, fixed the date for the executions, arranged for the noose and finally hired the hangman, just to give the final touch by pulling the lever for a small reward....
>
> The Nellie massacre, as we have observed elsewhere, provides clear insights to the political scientist and to the sociologist that a social movement, though ideologically based on secular issues, may turn non-secular in expression. (Hussain 1993: 142)

Such an argument implies that there was no real confrontation between the Muslim peasants and the indigenous and low-caste Assamese neighbors, but the disturbance was created by the middle-class movement leaders. This type of argument sees the entire Nellie incident as manipulation by the AASU and the AAGSP.

On the other hand, a few others have pointed out that the Nellie incident was "retaliation" by the Tiwas who had been deprived of their land by the Muslims. For example, Sanjoy Hazarika wrote:

> Their bitterness grew as they saw the immigrants nourish the soil and grow more crops, making profits on fields which were, until recently, their own....

All roads led to Nellie as the Tiwas, their resentments growing, sharpened their daos, oiled their muskets and twanged their bows and arrows, preparing for what they regarded as judgement day. Perhaps it would be better described as pay-back day. (Hazarika 2001: 46)

Such a description is based on the assumption that the Tiwas were autonomous in their decision in attacking their Muslim neighbors.

The leadership and the issue of agency of the riot participants are very important issues in the study of collective violence in contemporary South Asia. As has been argued (Chapters 1–2) in this book, studies on the recent Hindu–Muslim communal riots by Paul Brass, for example, takes the view that such incidents are "produced" by large-scale Hindu right organizations. On the other hand, the studies by the Subaltern Studies Group focused on peasant insurgency in the colonial period. For example, Gyanendra Pandey, in his article which analyzed peasant insurgency against zamindars and talukdars in Awadh, wrote:

So, in the case of colonial India, the peasants have generally been treated as beneficiaries (economically) or an increasingly benevolent system or victims of an oppressive one, 'manipulated' (politically) by self-seeking politicians or 'mobilized' by large-hearted, selfless ones. Both viewpoints miss out an essential feature—the whole area of independent thought and conjecture and speculation (as well as action) on the part of the peasant. (Pandey 1982: 188)

He further stated,

It was not, thus, an abstract question of whom the Congress might choose as ally, and then educate and train for political action. The peasants of Awadh had already taken the lead in reaching out for an alliance. (Pandey 1982: 189)

However, Pandey stated that the collective violence which had taken place since the 1980s, particularly those under the category of "Hindu–Muslim communal riots," had taken new forms, as argued in Chapter 1. I quote again,

Sectarian violence in the 1980s appears to have taken on new and increasingly horrifying forms…the worst instances of recent violence…have amounted to pogroms, organized massacres in which large crowds of hundreds, thousands, and even, in places, tens of thousands have attacked the houses and property and lives of small, isolated, and previously identified members of the "other" community. (Pandey 1992: 46)

Figure 4.1
Resistance against Oppressors/Colonizers

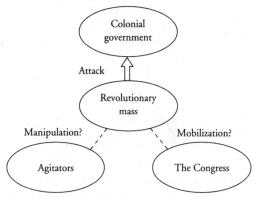

Figure 4.2
"Hindu–Muslim Communal Violence": Involvement of Large-Scale Organizations

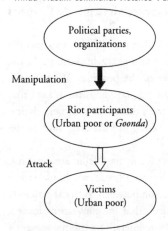

There is certainly a change in the social structure from the colonial period. The peasant insurgencies in the colonial period were resistance by the subalterns against the power-holders. However, in the so-called Hindu–Muslim communal riots which became prominent since the 1980s, it was not the poor or the peasants against the power-holders, but the poor against the poor, backed by political parties or large-scale religious or ethnic organizations. Let us illustrate the two models (Figures 4.1 and 4.2).

Figure 4.3
The Nellie Incident

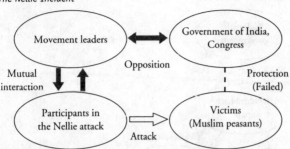

Does the Nellie incident fit into one of these two models?

The Nellie incident is certainly closer to the second model. However, there are certain differences such that we cannot categorize the Nellie massacre in it. First of all, apart from the attackers, the student leaders, and the victims, we have to take into consideration the fourth factor: the Congress party which held power at the center.

From my fieldwork, it can be pointed out that it is difficult to conclude that the incident was created solely by the middle-class leadership. At the same time, it was not only by the initiative of the peasants. Without the antiforeigner movement, the incident would not have happened. I see that the incident took place in the process of the interaction and negotiation between the student leaders and the local residents of the area, such as the Tiwas and the Kochs.

In this perspective (Figure 4.3), the violence in the Nellie area was not only manipulated by the student leaders at the top. Instead, we should rather see it as a product of negotiation and interaction between the local residents and the movement leaders. It is certainly true that the movement leaders provided the ideology of driving out the "foreigners," by the movement's slogans. At the same time, the villagers who suffered land alienation at the hands of the Muslims interpreted "foreigners" as "Muslims of East Bengal" origin, or more precisely, as *miyas*.

Thus, the Tiwas and the Kochs also interpreted the movement and its ideology in a way which suited their interests, and used it to attack the Muslims whom they felt were disturbing their lives seriously. The movement leaders utilized such a situation, or at least were in connivance with it in the process of raising support and cooperation to the election boycott. Such a structure of labeling the Muslims as the "enemy" had already been established in 1980 when there was an attack against the Muslims in the North Kamrup area. In this way, the movement leaders and the local residents in the Nellie area collaborated in the attack.

To see the Nellie incident as a product of interaction between the movement leaders and the local residents, rather than to specify either of them as solely responsible in the attack, would give us some advantage. First of all, by focusing on the relationship between the two, we would be able to analyze the tension between the two actors without overlooking the agency of the attackers in the violence. Although it was true that the movement had a significant impact in triggering the attack, there was indeed a decision-making process among the Tiwas and the local residents, as will be argued in the next chapter.

Moreover, the model I presented does not overlook the responsibilities of the movement leaders, the AASU and the AAGSP, as well as the Congress government at the center. Although the Tiwa and the Koch roles in the attack cannot be denied, it should be remembered that the movement leaders provided the legitimacy and the ideology to recognize the Muslims as "foreigners," who were taking their lands away, and portrayed them as "enemies." The blame should go to the Congress government, which failed to provide a constructive solution to the issue of immigration and foreign nationals in Assam. Instead, some of the politicians in the party instigated violence with inflammable speech as will be shown later in this chapter. The breakdown of order in the state not only threatened minorities, but also the supporters of the movement who saw that when the Congress won, they would become a "minority" in their own state.

What should be recalled while considering the agency of the attackers of the Nellie massacre is that at the time of the incident, the Tiwas and the Kochs in the area had limited options due to the political confrontation and crisis created by the movement leaders and the Congress government. Those who participated in the attack saw it as an opportunity to take back their land from the Muslims of immigrant origin. At the same time, they also felt threatened that if they did not attack the Muslims, the latter would come and attack. In studies on riots, it has been pointed out that the sense of self-defence is strong among riot participants (Horowitz 2001: 74–75; Spencer 2003: 1571).

Two Commission Reports and the Role of the Congress Government

The Politics of Interpreting Violence: Appointment of an Official Inquiry Commission

After the election and the Nellie incident, the GOI, the AASU and other civil society organizations, as well as the media, started to give comments, critiques, and explanations regarding the violence. The GOI put the blame on the AASU for the boycott and for provoking violence. The AASU and the AAGSP criticized the government for imposing an election which resulted in grave violence. This resulted in blame displacement to locate who was responsible for the disturbance. It is palpable that there should have been a struggle for control over the interpretation of communal riots in India, beginning with the different parties involved in the violence. Brass points out that after the riot, there always emerges a constant struggle to control the meaning of riots. Moreover, such interpretation itself will influence, or even determine power relations in society thereafter—relations among groups, within groups, and between the state and the society (Brass 2003: 21–22). Thus, in order to analyze the reports and comments produced after the violence, we need to keep in mind not only the examination of facts stated in the documents, but also put them into the larger context of what political stakes the documenter of the report had.

Regarding the election disturbance in Assam in 1983, not only the movement leaders and supporters in Assam, but also the mainstream media, were critical of the role of the GOI in imposing the election. For example, before the Assam election, there was heightened anxiety that it would result in bloodshed. Shekhar Gupta, an *Indian Express* correspondent, posed such a question when he interviewed a Congress member of parliament. The reply was, he recalled, "If you put 5,000 of them in jail for the election period, the problem is solved" (Gupta 1984: 29–30).

When Indira Gandhi visited Nellie after the incident, she faced the question of whether or not the GOI was responsible. She said, "No, the students and the agitators were to blame; they had created a climate of violence by spurning talks with the Government" (Hazarika 2001: 52).

Arun Shourie, editor of the *Indian Express,* published a long report on the disturbance, particularly regarding the Nellie incident. In examining police reports and internal information, Shourie pointed out three things. First, before the election, ensuring a free and fair poll was not the priority for the police and administrative officers, as well as security personnel. For them, the goal was not "to be able to hold the elections," but "to be able to proclaim one way or another that the ritual of the elections had been gone through." Thus, the police and security personnel were made to concentrate on the polling booths in order to protect the 8,000 officers who had been airlifted for polling duty, and the candidates and their families (Shourie 1983: 32).

Another important thing pointed out by him was that local policemen were not satisfied with the center's decision, and they became very hostile towards the state apparatus. There was obvious hostility between the local Assam police and the CRPF personnel, who were brought into the area in order to assist the local police. At one place, the hostility erupted into an open battle between the Assam Police and the CRPF.

Last, regarding the Nellie incident, there was a wireless message sent on February 15, 1983, only three days before the incident, by the Nagaon Police Station that warned of a possible attack in the area. The village residents had visited the officer-in-charge of the Nagaon Police Station, Zahirud Din Ahmed, and requested him to take some action. This showed that there was a specific warning from the district headquarters to the police station in Jagiroad, but that the concerned officers failed to take any action (Shourie 1983).

Faced with criticism, the Congress government had to somehow respond to these questions. In July 1983, five months after the incident, the Government of Assam appointed a retired Indian Administrative Service (IAS) officer, T. P. Tewary, to investigate the matter in response. His task was to inquire and report on the following matters: (1) to look into the circumstances leading to the disturbances; (2) to examine the measures taken by the concerned authorities and assess their adequacy; and (3) to suggest measures to prevent the recurrence of such incidents in future (Reproduced in Tewary Commission Report 1984: 411).

The Commission members visited some of the major trouble spots including Nellie. Apart from inquiring with local communities, their major task was to examine major government officials such as deputy commissioners, superintendents of police, and divisional commissioners, as well as other low- and high-ranking officials. The Commission completed the report and it was printed in May 1984. It was not, however, made public,[4] and so far, the outcome has not been examined by civil society.[5]

The movement leaders, having asked to hold a judicial inquiry into the disturbance, decided to boycott the Tewary Commission. Instead, Asom Rajyik Freedom Fighters Association decided to constitute a nonofficial judicial inquiry commission. They appointed T. U. Mehta (a retired chief justice of the High Court of Himachal Pradesh), and two Assamese, G. C. Phukan (retired IAS) and Raihan Shah (retired professor of Cotton College, Guwahati) to enquire into the disturbances before, during, and after the State Legislative Assembly election in Assam from January to April 1983.

Both the Tewary Commission Report and the Mehta Commission Report do not provide any details regarding the attackers involved in the collective violence. The role of the top leaders of the AASU or the AAGSP in any of the incidents has not been established beyond reports in newspapers, weekly journals, and other publications. However, the two reports provide statistics regarding the incidents and casualties at the time. As quoted earlier in this chapter, the number of incidents and casualties according to police reports are provided in the Tewary Commission Report. On the other hand, more than 70 incidents of ethnic clashes are outlined in the Mehta Commission Report, providing information regarding which communities in which areas were targeted. In sum, these provide basic information for understanding the overall situation regarding the collective violence that took place during the State Legislative Assembly election in Assam in 1983.

At the same time, both the commissions were, from the beginning, biased towards certain organizations, and their work was utilized to show the GOI's and student leaders' perspectives. It is regrettable that there has been no neutral and third-party investigation regarding the Nellie incident and other disturbances that took place in the first three months of 1983, such as the ones conducted by the People's Union for Democratic Rights or the People's Union for Civil Liberties in regard to other incidents. The absence of such an investigation prevents us from understanding important aspects of the Nellie incident.

The Role of the Congress Government

The relationship between movement leaders and riot participants has been already discussed in this chapter. In order to understand some of the factors leading to the Nellie incident, however, it is essential to examine the role of the Congress government as well. The violence would not have taken place without the boycott by the AASU and the AAGSP. At the same time, it can be pointed out that the Congress prioritized its interests, and that some of its top leaders instigated violence rather than pursuing their duty to hold a fair and safe election.

LEGITIMACY FOR HOLDING ELECTION

The question whether it was necessary to hold an election at the time had been raised even before the election. The Congress government claimed that it was necessary to hold a State Legislative Assembly election citing Article 356 of the Constitution of India, which states that President's rule cannot be extended beyond a period of one year. However, there were some measures available to postpone it. One way was to amend the Constitution, which was not impossible at the time. Otherwise, the

> President's rule in Assam could have been extended beyond March 19, 1983, if: (*a*) a Proclamation of Emergency was declared for the State of Assam, and (*b*) the Election Commission certified that on account of difficulties of holding general elections in Assam, continuation of the President's rule was necessary. (Mehta Commission Report 1985: 53)

The Congress government had its own reason to forcefully implement the election in order to hold power in the state. The party had already lost in the State Legislative Assembly elections in Karnataka and Tripura, and was keen on winning the election in Assam. As the AASU and the AAGSP had already declared their rejection of any election without the revision of electoral rolls, the Congress was confident that it would gain the majority of the votes. Although the Election Commission had once promised not to hold elections without revising the rolls, under government pressure it failed to refuse the election. Even the Election Commission had admitted that "the situation in Assam is not absolutely ideal for holding an election" (Mehta Commission Report 1985: 36).

INSTIGATION OF VIOLENCE BY A CONGRESS POLITICIAN

Another issue was that some politicians acted provocatively just before the election. One important allegation was against A. Ghani Khan Choudhury, railway minister at the time. In the first half of February, he visited Nagaon and other districts with Prime Minister Indira Gandhi. Being a Bengali Muslim, he visited areas where the Muslims of immigrant origin lived, a solid vote bank for the Congress, and made inflammatory speeches in Bengali language. One part of his speech that became controversial was when he said, "If Hindus kill one Muslim, the Muslims should retaliate by killing two (or three). The Government would support you."

In my fieldwork in the Nellie area, several people referred to Choudhury's visit to the Muslim-dominated area in Nagaon as one factor causing tension in the region.[6] This is also recorded in the Mehta Commission Report. One of Choudhury's speeches was taperecorded and submitted to the Commission. There were several witnesses to prove that he made this speech (Mehta Commission Report 1985: 39–40).

The Congress' assurance that they would back the Muslims of Bengali origin created fear among the local Assamese who supported the movement and the AASU. Such instigation by a Congress politician shows that the tension in the area was not only created by the AASU's boycott, but also by an important politician of the ruling party.

DYSFUNCTION OF LAW-ENFORCEMENT AGENCIES

The Tewary Commission investigated the two points raised by Shourie in his report: a wireless message that had warned of possible attack in the Nellie area, and the negligence of the local police. Regarding a wireless message sent by the Nagaon Police Station to the 5th Assam Police Battalion camp, all three officers-in-charge denied receiving the message. The report concluded that it was "bewildering" that none of them admitted to having received the message before the event (Tewary Commission Report 1984: 307).

The commission also looked into some dubious acts of the officer-in-charge of Jagiroad Police Station. Although he had received information regarding the attack at about 10:35 a.m. on February 18, he did not proceed to the villages where the attacks had taken place and instead started rescuing people drowning in the Kopili River. The officer's excuse was that he did not know a suitable path from Nellie to the attacked villages (Muladhari and Mati-Parbot). The commission did not consider his evidence reliable at all and concluded:

In the case of the Nellie incident, what is established is that the force that was available with the officer-in-charge of the Jagiroad Police Station on the 17th and then on the 18th of February, 1983, was not utilized effectively and immediately on receiving the information. (Tewary Commission Report 1984: 309–11)

The third point is essential to understanding the factors that made it possible for the villagers to attack their neighbors. If the law-enforcement agencies were functioning, it would have been impossible for them to riot. At that time, the police and security forces were defunct for two reasons: (1) the number of security officers available was not enough. As Shourie has pointed out, the CRPF and other armed police battalions were brought in from other states, but they were mainly posted in polling booths and to provide security for election candidates. (2) The Assam Police personnel, especially low-ranking officers, were sympathetic to the movement and did not take measures to prevent attacks in some areas. Regarding the Nellie incident in particular, the local police did not take any action despite knowing that the attack was taking place.

Some of the leaders who planned the attack must have had information that the local police would not work against them. In the case of other large-scale riots, the government is usually sympathetic to the attackers and does not take effective measures to stop the violence. What was unique regarding the Nellie incident was that the local police did not obey the government order to intervene because of the strong influence of the movement leaders. In this case, the government's failure was in its lack of ability to control the police when enforcing an election that invited opposition from every corner.

Concluding Remarks

Many issues are raised as factors that led to the group clashes and mass killings—immigration, loss of land, a forced election, and the AASU's or Congress's instigation. In the analysis of collective violence in contemporary South Asia, the question "who was responsible for the violence?" can be tricky. One of the main aims of this book is to analyze how "ordinary people" participate in large-scale violence like the Nellie incident. It is my perspective that the attackers in the Nellie massacre were not mere puppets completely controlled by political parties or large-scale organizations. As will be discussed in the following chapters, the Tiwa, Koch, and other Assamese Hindu villagers had their own reasons and decision-making processes in attacking their Muslim neighbors. At the same time, it is also misleading to put the responsibility and the blame of the violence solely on them. In order to understand the context which led to the attack, together with the structural causes such as immigration and land issues, we need to understand the roles played by the government and the movement leaders.

In this regard, the first and foremost cause was the GOI's failure in handling the situation skilfully and, to some extent, the AASU's failure. The State Legislative Assembly election became an occasion for both the Congress and the AASU to pursue success in their attempt to hold control in Assam, and thus, the two powerful organizations' interests clashed.

The antiforeigner movement, which lasted more than four years at the time of the election, resulted in the marginalization of the Muslims of East Bengal origin. They were easily targeted as "foreigners" and thus felt threatened. The "otherization" of the Muslims had a significant impact in targeting them as foreigners, and as a result, they became victims of the violence. The AASU leaders not only failed to stop this violence when it broke out, but they also let some of their leaders lend a hand in the attack mainly against the Muslims.

On the other hand, the Congress-led government forced the election in order to establish a Congress government in the state. To make full use of this opportunity, the government neglected warnings by police and intelligence officers of the possibility of violence, and concentrated police and security personnel in the polling booths. This attitude invited hostility among the local police personnel against the election and partly resulted in their negligence to prevent the violence.

To sum up, both the AASU and the GOI did not make enough effort to prevent the violence that had easily been predicted. Instead, both parties tried to utilize the opportunity to gain power to their own end. In this way, both of them cannot escape the criticism of instigating small-scale violence and creating an atmosphere where everybody felt threatened of their security. By creating such situation, the options of the masses, particularly that of the minority people were limited. For the Tiwas and the Kochs, the attack was rather a retaliation or preemptive attack to a possible offensive by the Muslims.

Notes

1. A nonviolent disobedience movement which was started by Mahatma Gandhi during the
   nationalist movement.
2. A military-style rush that uses *lathi*, a six- to eight-foot (2.4 m) long cane tipped with an
   optional metal blunt, it is often used by the Indian police to disperse crowds.
3. This figure has been estimated on the basis of the 1971 census.
4. A copy is in the State Legislative Assembly Library. So officially, only MLAs are eligible to
   read the document. The author obtained a photostat copy through an anonymous source.
   Although it was not officially published, many people including the former AASU and
   AAGSP leaders have seen the report.
5. In 2009, Teresa Rehman published a part of the report in a weekly magazine (Rehman
   2009).
6. For example, an interview with an elderly Tiwa person in Parahguri village, November 12,
   2001.

5

Agency of the Rioters: A Study of Decision Making in the Nellie Massacre*

There are still a number of unexplained factors in the phenomenon called "riot," which is a particular form of collective violence enacted by a section of the civilian populace against another. The most prominent among them are: why do ordinary people attack their neighbors or colleagues with whom they have shared long social relationships, and furthermore, how do they go back to their normal lives after the episode of violence?

The past two decades have seen a number of studies—in history, political science, and sociology—on the phenomenon of collective violence in India, or the so-called communal riot. In the areas of political science and sociology, it is a common understanding that violence in urban areas in India has become routine, and in order to analyze it, we need to study political and social systems or institutions, which need communal riots in order to exist.

As stated in Chapter 1, though there is no arguing that the routinization of violence is a serious phenomenon in parts of India, especially in the north, there have been cases where violence was not only manipulated by politicians and perpetrated by *goondas* or criminal elements, but also by "ordinary people" who participated in such attacks. This is usually at the time of political transformation and the large-scale breakdown of law and order. The Nellie massacre, which took place in Assam in 1983, was one such incident.

The aim of this chapter is not to specify the root cause or the sole reason for the attack, but to analyze how the riot participants understood these factors when they made their decision to engage in violence. There are competing, and sometimes contradicting, narratives on the incident, and a close look at the complicated and sometimes fragmented accounts by the riot participants gives us a richer understanding of the phenomenon. It leads to a new and nuanced understanding of the rural impact of the antiforeigner movement in Assam.

* Reproduced with permission from *Beyond Counter-insurgency: Breaking the Impasse in Northeast India*; Sanjib Baruah, New Delhi©2009, published by Oxford University Press India.

Nellie: History of Immigration and Alienation of Tribal Land

As with most territories that are contested by different communities, there is a need to understand the socioeconomic history of the land that is being fought over. The site of the incident, Nellie, is situated between Guwahati, the political center of Assam and Nagaon, a district headquarter in central Assam. At the time of the incident, the area was under the jurisdiction of Nagaon District, but later, in the mid-1980s, the districts in Assam were reorganized and it came under the newly constituted Morigaon District.

As with much of Assam, the erstwhile undivided district of Nagaon was predominantly rural. Prior to colonization, there existed a Tiwa kingdom called Gobha, which was located between Guwahati and the town of Nagaon. Nellie is close to the erstwhile capital of the kingdom and thus there is a substantial Tiwa population in the area. In 1,905, before the immigration started, the Tiwas comprised more than 10 percent of the population of the district.[1] The main crops grown in the district were jute and rice, and both were cultivated predominantly by the Muslims of East Bengal origin. Their numerical strength in the district comes from a long, well-documented colonial policy that was enacted by the British in the early 20th century. According to this policy, the Bengali-speaking Muslim peasants from districts like Mymensingh, were allowed to come and settle in parts of the Brahmaputra valley. In the 1920s and the 1930s, the Muslim settlers first started to settle down in the areas close to the banks of the Brahmaputra River, which constitutes the northern border of the district. According to the 1971 census, 39.39 percent of the population of the district was Muslim, and most of them were descendants of immigrants from Mymensingh. In 2001, the number of Muslims exceeded half the population in both Morigaon and Nagaon Districts.

According to C. S. Mullan, superintendent of census operation in Assam, Nowgong (Nagaon) was "conquered" by the "land-hungry Bengali immigrants, mostly Muslims" from 1921 to 1931 (Census of India 1931: 49–52). Furthermore, in the report from Nowgong, he is quoted as having written:

> The increase in population is especially noticeable in Khathowal, Juria, Laokhowa, Dhing, Bokoni and Lahorighat mauzas when it is solely due to the large influx of immigrant settlers mainly from Mymensingh. They have opened

up vast tracts of dense jungle along the south bank of the Brahmaputra and
have occupied nearly all the lands which are open for settlement in this tract....

Immigration in recent years mainly signifies the influx into this district of
Mahomedan [Muslims] and Hindu families from the Eastern Bengal districts,
chiefly from Mymensingh. They had begun to come in large numbers from
the latter part of the previous decade but their numbers gradually continued
to swell every year till 1926 when there was a slight decrease in the flow on
account of the fact that almost all the areas originally assigned to them were
already occupied leaving little room for further extention and also because
they were attracted by new lands made available in other districts. (Census
of India 1931: 49–52)

This account also refers to the friction which occurred between the Muslim
migrants and the indigenous population over the issue of land.

Their [Muslims] hunger for land was so great that, in their eagerness to grasp as
much as they could cultivate, they not infrequently encroached on Government
reserves and on lands belonging to the local people, from which they could
be evicted only with great difficulties. In the beginning they had their own
way and there was frequent friction with the indigenous population who did
not like their dealings as neighbours. The appointment of special colonisa-
tion officer and adoption of certain definite rules tended much to regularise
settlement and prevent friction. (Census of India 1931: 51–52)

Table 5.1 shows the number of immigrants who came to Assam from
districts in Bengal. The figures of the Nowgong (Nagaon) District, show a
tremendous increase within a couple of decades—from 4,000 in 1911 to
120,000 in 1931. This clearly shows that in the 1920s, there was large-scale
immigration from districts in Bengal, especially Mymensingh.

Table 5.1
Number of Persons Born in Bengal District in Each District of the Assam Valley in 1911, 1921, and 1931

Year	Goalpara	Kamrup	Darrang	Nowgong	Sibsagar	Lakhimpur
1911	77,000	4,000	7,000	4,000	14,000	14,000
1921	151,000	44,000	20,000	58,000	14,000	14,000
1931	170,000	134,000	41,000	120,000	12,000	19,000

Source: Census of India 1931.

Nellie had fewer immigrants in the initial years. However, by the 1940s, the number of immigrants kept increasing and land became scarce in the northern part of the district. Political demands were made by the Muslim League, a party that was mainly backed by Muslim immigrants, to abolish the Line System[2] and open up some of the government land such as the Professional Grazing Reserves (PGRs) to accommodate immigrants. In 1943, after forming the fourth ministry under Saadulla, the Muslim League provincial government appointed S. P. Desai, a senior Indian Civil Service officer, as Special Officer to ascertain what portion of PGRs could be declared as surplus available for settlement. Desai reported that the forcible occupation of grazing lands by immigrants had already taken place at a large scale, even in the predominantly Assamese or tribal areas. His conclusion was that there was no surplus land available for new settlement. Ignoring the report, however, Saadulla's Muslim League coalition government threw select PGRs open for settling immigrants (Das 1986: 34; Guha 1977: 281–82).

Such historical notes are important in understanding the conflict, when it finally came to occur in the 1980s. The villages attacked in the Nellie incident were part of a PGR called Alichinga Grazing Reserve, and it was opened to immigrants in 1943.[3] Presently, there are 9–10 villages on the location, and all of them were the target of attack in the Nellie incident (Map 5.1).

Thus, we can see that the villages affected by the Nellie incident came into existence in the 1940s under the Muslim League government's "Grow More Food" policy, and that right from the beginning, the existence of these villages was controversial in terms of whether the new settlement of immigrants should be allowed or not. The policy was in fact described by some as a "Grow More Muslims" policy, and led to confrontation between the Assamese and Bengali immigrants.

For the Tiwas, the immigration which started in the 1920s and the 1930s marked the beginning of the loss of their traditional land. Having their origins in the hill areas,[4] they continued to practice shifting cultivation even after they migrated to the plains. The British colonial officers had introduced the private land ownership system in Assam in the late 19th century, which worked adversely for the indigenous peoples, including the Tiwas. Primarily shifting cultivators, they did not choose to take a periodical lease of their lands and preferred the annual lease, continuing to shift their agricultural land frequently. Meanwhile, immigrants who were keen on taking periodical leases had bought land from them. The British colonial administrators called the shifting cultivation "fluctuating cultivation" and saw it as an outdated

Map 5.1

Grazing Reserves of Nowgong (Nagaon) District (Including Alichinga Grazing Reserve), 1944

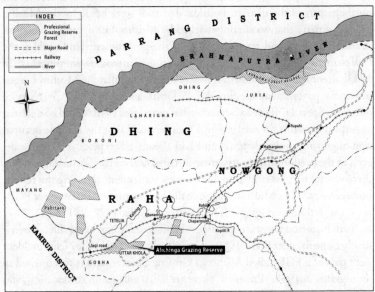

Source: Report of the Special Officer Appointed for the Examination of the Professional Grazing Reserves in the Assam Valley, 1944.

and ineffective way to utilize the land; they thus thought of abolishing it in due course and encouraged the intensive cultivation practiced by the Muslim immigrants. Such a situation is described in *Report of the Line System Committee* published in 1938. Sanjib Baruah states that after the immigrants from the East Bengal settled in the riverine areas, the shifting cultivation by the Assamese peasants[5] disappeared (Baruah 2005: 91).

When indigenous tribes like the Tiwa suffered dramatic losses of land and resources following large-scale immigration into Nagaon, the colonial authorities began to talk about protective measures to prevent further losses. This proposal was included in the resolution by the Line System Committee's report, and finally Tribal Belts and Blocks were created in 1946 (Das 1986: 35–37). Non-tribal persons were prohibited from settling in the Tribal Belts and Blocks.[6] It may be mentioned here that the area just north of the villages that were attacked in February 1983, were also specified as a tribal block called Tetelia Tribal Block, meant for the Tiwa community, in 1950 (Bordoloi 1999: 14).

On the other hand, immigrants who were subjected to exploitative treatment under the *zamindari* system in East Bengal, particularly those from Mymensingh District, were hardworking cultivators accustomed to intensive cultivation and a cash economy. Here is an account of the immigrants in Laharighat *Mauza*,[7] which was one of the areas where the immigrants became dominant in the 1930s. This illustrates well the difference between the immigrant Muslims and the local Assamese, including indigenous tribal groups such as the Tiwa:

> The Assamese are un-ambitious and are easily satisfied. They do not usually go in for debts; small amounts which they might borrow are quickly repaid after harvest. The immigrants are however habitual borrowers. They spend a lot of money recklessly in litigation, good houses, cattle and dress and for buying more land. In normal years they clear off their debts. When they want money they do not hesitate even to execute bonds for double the amount they actually borrow. (Mauza Note Laharighat 1931: page number not indicated)

Although the colonial trope of "lazy natives," prevalent in this quotation, lacks an understanding of the traditional culture and way of life, it also illustrates the situation where the Muslims were successful in adapting to changes brought about by colonization while the Tiwas became the losers. It has been alleged that the Muslims often harassed local populations to grab land, but the enquiry of the Line System Committee reveals that although there were such cases, the allegations were largely exaggerated (Report of the Line System Committee 1938: 18).

According to the report, the Tiwas inhabited the area north of the Alichinga Grazing Reserve in Tetelia Mauza. Due to the large tribal concentration, the area was declared a "tribal block" immediately after independence. As per the laws laid down for areas reserved as tribal blocks, non-tribal people were prohibited from obtaining land and even today, the area continues to be home to a tribal majority. However, the prohibition was not strictly enforced in most places and in many areas, non-tribals continued to acquire land in the blocks.

Thus, from the analysis of documents on grazing reserves and tribal blocks, we can point out that Nellie and its contiguous villages, were one of the areas where the immigrants started to settle in the 1940s. While the immigrants were fast acquiring land, the indigenous tribal groups were gradually losing control over their traditionally inhabited land in the district.

However, there is a problem with this simplistic narrative, where the indigenous communities solely hold immigrants responsible for the loss of land. In fact, the British government played a role in bringing the immigrants for the purpose of increasing land revenue. Thus, the cause-and-effect link between the immigrants' settlement and the alienation of tribes from their traditional land needs much more careful investigation. Here, we can only suggest that the areas in which the Nellie massacre took place were also areas in which there had been major disputes in the 1940s. These disputes had to do with whether or not to open the land to the immigrants, and the area also had a fairly large number of Tiwa villages.

The situation had not changed much even in the 1980s. It has been reported that the Tiwas in the area often sold land due to their indebtedness to the moneylenders who often belong to the immigrant communities. The moneylenders charged exorbitant interest for money that they lent out to the Tiwas for illnesses and ceremonies. Many were therefore unable to pay back their loans and as a result of this, they sold their lands and became agricultural laborers or moved to other areas. Such a situation was prevalent even in the tribal blocks where the transaction of land to non-tribals is illegal (Sharma Thakur 1986: 101–2).

When the antiforeigner movement started, the movement's leaders raised the issue of land alienation among the indigenous communities in order to back their claims that the influx of foreigners created socioeconomic problems in Assam. Considering the history of the area and the problem of land alienation among the indigenous peoples, it is not surprising that when the violence broke out many academics and journalists cited land alienation among them as a root cause of the violence. There were, however, other proximate reasons behind the violence.

Narratives of the Rioters

The analysis in this chapter is based on fieldwork conducted in November 2001 and February 2002. These include several group interviews with villagers who joined the attack and the local leaders in the Nellie area. Interviews were also conducted with local leaders of the antiforeigner movement, who joined the All Assam Students' Union (AASU) and the All Assam Gana Sangram Parishad (AAGSP) in Jagiroad and Morigaon, local towns near Nellie. I was successful in interviewing those who joined the attack: the Tiwas, the Kochs, and the caste-Hindu Assamese. The survivors, who were descendants of the immigrant Muslims from Bengal, were more reluctant than the attackers to speak about the incident. I visited Nellie and its adjoining areas again in 2007 and at that time, I was successful in talking to the Muslims and getting their views on the events, including the attack where several thousand men, women, and children were killed.

Contrary to my expectation that those who joined the attack would not be willing to talk about the incident, it was not very difficult to find informants from amongst the Tiwas, the Kochs, and the Hiras. Some of the Tiwa respondents particularly, were very vocal. The reason for the difference will be analyzed in the next chapter and the conclusion, as it has more relevance to the issues of "memory." Here, my focus is mainly on the decision-making process, which led to the large-scale killing.

The villagers who joined the attack cited several factors, which they believed to be the motivational causes of the attack. These factors were often contradictory to each other. Moreover, the villagers did not refer to land alienation as the primary cause of the incident. Other factors, such as the disputed elections of 1983, the AASU movement and their leadership, and periodic occurrences of small-scale trouble, such as allegations of kidnapping of girls, were cited as the main causes for the attack.

Lack of "Land Alienation" in the Narratives

As noted, the existing literature attributed land alienation as the primary cause of the incident. Before the interviews with the villagers, I expected that there must have been some problems regarding land between the Muslims and the Tiwas, the Kochs, and the other Assamese Hindus. However, contrary to my expectation, the interviewees did not mention any trouble with respect to their land, during the group interviews with them. In one group interview, this was one of the counterintuitive responses:

> We did not have any confrontation with Muslims. We had good relations with them. We exchanged our agricultural products.[8]

And in another:

> We did not have any troubles before the incident. We had peaceful relations
> with Muslims.[9]

The impact of land alienation among the indigenous groups, including
the Tiwas, was felt more in the northern part of Nagaon District where the
Muslim population was considerably larger. In 1983, in the southern part of
the district, where the Nellie incident took place, the Tiwas, the Kochs and
other Hindus outnumbered the Muslims, who were scattered throughout
different pockets in the area. In fact, the Tiwa and Koch villages surrounded
the ten Muslim villages attacked in the incident.

In the 1960s, due to an increase in population, the Muslims in the northern part of the district began migrating to southern parts of Nagaon and also
to other districts. The impact of erosion near the bank of the Brahmaputra
River caused a lot of damage and several villages were completely washed
away, thereby increasing the pressure to migrate for those based in proxim-
ity to the river in north Nagaon. Many Muslim villagers became landless
and they came to Morigaon, Jagiroad, and villages in the southern part, in
search of jobs and land. It is a fact that the Muslim population was growing
in Nellie as well. However, the interviews show that the threat of pressure
for land was not acutely felt till the movement started.

On the other hand, there were testimonies that attested to the benefits of
attacking the Muslims. For instance, it was believed that, "if you attack the
Muslims and drive them out, you can obtain their land."[10] Considering
the socioeconomic structure of the area, it can be analyzed that rather than
the land alienation, some local people in the area saw the antiforeigner movement and the disturbance caused by the election as a good chance to drive
out the Muslims in order to appropriate their land.

Tension between the Muslims and the Attackers

Although the villagers denied troubles regarding land, some of them mentioned that there were other kinds of troubles with the Muslims. In a group
interview in one village, an elderly person was very vocal about the issue of
kidnapping of girls:

Initially, we were living peacefully. But one point was noticed by us later on, that many girls were kidnapped and they used to kill them.... They used to take girls; they used to keep them at their homes and some of them they used to kill. We were very much offended, and this thing was shared with the AASU and the Assamese people from these areas.... The main issue was girls.... This thing came to light in 1982–83, but it was happening silently.[11]

In the narratives on collective violence, there are often cases of attacks targeting children and women being emphasized as a reason for retaliation. When, in particular, the enemy is defined along ethnic/religious lines, children and women are taken as community "property" and any harm to them attempted is regarded as a threat to the whole community.

In another village, a villager noted in an interview that there were troubles regarding cows:

There were cases that several cows crossed the river and went to Muladhari (one of the attacked villages). Muslims kill and eat cows. (Ajarbari village, November 24, 2001)

There were several similar testimonies that claimed that the Muslim villagers stole cows and other agricultural products, and that these small-scale incidents caused friction between the Muslims and their neighbors in adjacent villages. These small-scale alleged skirmishes between the Muslims and their tribal neighbors, however, were told as a supplement to other factors and not as a primary cause of the incident. It was the elections, its boycott called by the AASU and the subsequent tension, which the villagers mentioned as the primary factors to begin rioting.

The image of the "land-hungry Mussalman," as caricatured in Mullan's census report, was often exaggerated and it was usually the case that the Tiwas, the Kochs, the Hiras, and other peasants had mortgaged their lands. However, it is also true that in the areas where the Muslims were a majority, such incidents had added to the threat perception of the Assamese people and indigenous communities.

Opposition towards the Congress Government

Along with complaints of small-scale disputes with the Muslim neighbors, some people spoke of the fear that the Muslims would grow to outnumber the local people on their own land. Many mentioned such fear in different ways, but the most typical manner was as follows:

> At the time, Congress politicians did not implement proper measures [on the issue of immigration]. That is why the AASU leaders began the antiforeigner movement. The Congress party was pro-Muslim, and Indira Gandhi, the party president at the time, took the same line. In this area, all the Hindus supported the movement.... Many Muslims came here. Their population was increasing because they have a larger number of children. For the Muslims, numbers are important.[12]

The above statement was made by a local AAGSP activist in the Nellie area. The fear of the Muslims becoming a population majority in the future is one heard often in interviews with local leaders or active members of the AASU and the AAGSP. Expressed in these narratives is a fear not only of the simple fact of being outnumbered, but also of the Assamese people possibly losing political power in their own state. Connected to this, people complain that the Congress government did not take effective measures, and instead protected the Muslims in order to gain power in the state. Such tone is more apparent in the following:

> We thought that if we lost, we would become foreigners in our own land....
> I felt the Assamese should have the sovereign right in Assam, but it was controlled by the Indians.[13]

This statement was made by a former active member of the AAGSP, an Assamese Muslim, who had been a teacher at a local school in the Nellie area at the time. The statement "I would become a foreigner in my own land" sounds extreme and without any rational reason. However, this person was categorized as a "doubtful voter"[14] in the electoral roll and could not cast a vote for a certain period. Such retaliation by the ruling party is not unheard of in politics in Assam.

At the time of the antiforeigner movement, dissatisfaction towards the Congress government, which could not control the number of immigrants and instead suppressed the AASU movement, was shared widely among the Assamese and indigenous tribal groups. Moreover, such antipathy towards the Congress was often directed towards the Muslims, their vote bank. Also, those who engaged in activities of the AASU and the AAGSP feared that the Congress would retaliate in some form against them if they lost.

However, the people actively engaged in the movement were the caste-Hindu Assamese or from the relatively educated segment of the Tiwas and other Hindus of lower strata. Not all the Tiwas and other local villagers in the Nellie area were active in the movement. For the villagers without a direct connection with the movement, antipathy towards the Congress or fear that the Muslims might outnumber them one day were not urgent issues. A more acute threat was decisive in their decision to riot.

AASU Leadership or Local Leadership?

Some of my respondents stated that the tension due to the election boycott called by the AASU triggered the attack. Among them, several villagers stressed that it was the AASU who started the incident, and not the Tiwas.

> It was led by the AASU. But they cheated. Everybody supported the movement.
>   All the villages, areas, societies and district supported. Actually we did not know why we had to boycott the election. They said the cause was (the) foreigner (agitation). And whenever they knew that (a) village was affected by this kind of troubles, (like) the [kidnap of] girls, so they triggered, means they said, "OK we will [support] you."[15]

Before jumping to a conclusion that it was the AASU who took the lead in the attack, we should examine who these "AASU leaders" were. In this area, those who were referred to as "AASU leaders" were students from this area who had been actively involved in the movement. The top AASU leadership in Guwahati or Nagaon had rarely visited this area. Even those involved in the AASU and the AAGSP in Morigaon did not have a clear idea as to where the villages that were attacked were located. It is unlikely that the movement leaders in the towns took the lead in the attack.

When I went through the villagers' narratives thoroughly, those who had been alleged to be (or sometimes had admitted themselves as) leading the attackers were those from neighboring villages who had been involved in the AASU and the AAGSP. Sometimes, it was also persons who had not participated in the antiforeigner movement actively, but who had seen the attack as a good chance to drive the Muslims away and appropriate their land. There were also a few local Congress supporters who had led the attack.

Moreover, there were meetings among the village leaders and elders, local leaders from the antiforeigner movement, and other men of influence, in order to decide whether they would join the attack or not. These were conducted jointly by several villages. These processes were clarified in my interviews with individuals who had been influential village leaders or local leaders involved in the movement. For instance, a leader of a Lalung (an old name for Tiwa) organization that was active at the time said that he had gone to one of those meetings and opposed the attacks.

> I went to a meeting held in Silchang one day before the attack. I insisted that we should not attack and we should protect ourselves, but most people disagreed with me.... There were rumors that in Nagaon or in Guwahati, Muslims are attacking the Assamese Hindus. Many people came from Morigaon and Kamrup and told us that they were attacked, so this time we should start attacking them (Muslims). There were also fears that killing took place in Muladhari.[16]

From his accounts it is known that there were several small-scale attacks during that time and that people felt that if they did not attack in advance, they would lose out to the Muslims. The fact that there was a meeting among the villagers shows that the attack was not spontaneous, and that there was a decision-making process through discussion among the local leaders and elders. From my enquiry, I learnt that such meetings had been held in several different localities in the Nellie area. The question arises, as there were people who opposed the attack, of what became a decisive factor in persuading them to participate in it.

Decision Making before the Attack

In order to look into the decision-making process that led to the attack on the Muslims, I would like to quote one long interview conducted in the Nellie area during my fieldwork in 2001. The person who gave me this account was a member of the Koch community, which is recognized as economically and socially backward in Assam. His village is located in the middle of the Tetelia Tribal Block, where 70 percent of the population are Koch, while the remaining 30 percent are Tiwa. At the time when the violence occurred, he was a first-year college student and an active AASU member of the locality. At the same time, he is a grandson of one of the founders of the village. His account shows the link between the movement and the decision to attack in the village.

According to him, in the villages in the Tetelia Tribal Block, the danger of the election disturbance was first felt by people when a disturbance took place in a village 10 km northwest to them. Prior to the Nellie incident, there was a rumor that Muslim outsiders had come to the area and that they had started harassing the Tiwa and Assamese peasants and were trying to grab their lands. He said,

> There were a few incidents before the Nellie incident took place. In a village called Gorjan, once upon a time the Tiwas were the majority of the residents. However, the number of Muslim peasants slowly increased and ultimately they became 80 percent of the population there. They damaged the crops in the Tiwa people's fields and tried to grab the land. At the time, there were a few cases of murder, I believe. As a result, a section of the Tiwa residents came to our village and planned to get back their land. They fought and were successful in regaining their land, but due to the fight 14–15 people died.[17]

In interviews conducted in a few other villages in the area, there are a number of accounts of the troubles and harassment meted out to the Tiwa and Assamese villagers by the Muslims. As noted in the section on tension, there were several allegations of kidnapping of girls, of the Muslims cultivating rice in fields belonging to the Assamese and the Tiwas, and of the Muslims letting loose cows in their fields. According to the former AASU activist, however, it was a more acute danger that led them to decide to attack the village.

> After the incident, many Muslims came from Gorjan to Muladhari [one of the attacked villages in the Nellie incident] and they left their wives and children in the village. Several Bihari fishermen who lived on the bank of the river Kopili came to know about their existence. They were threatened (and coerced) not to tell the others about them. However, the Muslims harassed the Bihari people. So they told us [the local villagers] that there are Muslims from Gorjan…. We felt scared to hear that the Muslims of Gorjan village had come to Muladhari. There were also cases where a few cows had crossed

the river and never returned. We suppose that the Muslims ate those cows. Thus, on February 13, the village elders held a meeting and discussed how to deal with them…. On February 14, the Muslims came to know about the meeting and they attacked the Bihari houses in retaliation. They burned down their houses at night. On the 15th, again the village elders assembled and we decided to attack the Muslims.

According to my source, leaders from several villages—Sonuabori, Pachalaghat, Mantabori, Silbeta, Borogaon—came to the meeting. It can be seen that despite being an AASU activist in the region, his narratives referred to the village elders as the key decision-makers in the attack. From his point of view it was not the AASU but the village elders who were the final decision-makers. His account continued as follows:

The hill Tiwa people had a good relationship with the plains Tiwa people. So we let them know about our attack. They agreed to participate in the attack and came down with handmade rifles and arrows one night before the attack…. First, we went to a village called Borbori across the national highway and killed 300 people there. After that, we crossed the highway and started attacking villages around Muladhari. That time, the villages were already surrounded from three corners. We started burning the houses at 11 a.m. and the attack continued till 3 p.m.

It has been argued that the tribes were merely utilized by the movement leaders or other miscreants who wanted to create disturbances, but there has not been much analysis on the decision-making process among the Tiwa and Assamese villagers. In the course of my interviews, it was clear that the decision-making process of the elders was a prominent motive in the attack. In riots that occurred in the rural areas of Nagaon during that period, the decision making among the village leaders should be considered as one of the important processes of the events leading to the violence. This is also very similar to what Beth Roy pointed out, in the process of decision making, in her study on the riot that took place in a rural area in erstwhile East Pakistan in 1954 (Roy 1994: 136).

If the meeting of the village elders was decisive in the initiative to start the riot, what was the point that tipped their decision? In order to answer this question, we have to examine the narrative, or rather the rumor, on the series of incidents which took place before the large-scale violence.

Interpreting the Narratives: The Role of Rumor

There is no arguing that a rumor on the series of incidents prior to the Nellie incident influenced the villagers in their decision to attack. The story consisted of the following incidents: (1) In a village, Gorjan, the Tiwas attacked the Muslims in retaliation for the loss of land and the harassment suffered. Prior to the incident the Tiwas had come to the respondent's village and planned the attack. (It can be suggested that the villagers in the interviewee's village had lent a hand in the attack.) The Tiwas got back some of their land. (2) After the first attack, the Muslims of Gorjan came to Muladhari, a neighboring Muslim village, and left their wives and children there. They also harassed the Biharis who lived on the border of the Muslim villages and the Assamese and Tiwa villages. (3) The first meeting on how to deal with the Muslims was held in the Tetelia Tribal Block. The Muslims, knowing about the meeting, attacked the Biharis and burned down their houses. (4) The village elders held a meeting and they decided to attack the Muslims.

How does one interpret this story? Is it a mere rumor that circulated before the riot, as many scholars suggest (Horowitz 2001; Pandey 2001; Spencer 2003)? Or is there any truth to it? It is clear from the interviewee's account that he was sure that such incidents really took place. Should we take his account to be the "truth," or as an event which was largely exaggerated?

At the time, there were many small-scale incidents, which took place all over Assam. Their frequency increased as the elections drew near. Just before violence erupted in Nellie, there was a report of the murder of Tiwa children in the Lahorighat area. The Lalung Darbar,[18] which submitted a memorandum to the prime minister, Indira Gandhi, just after the incident, noted several incidents that had occurred from February 12, 1983, to February 15, 1983, in Lahorighat and Mayang circles north of Nellie.

However, we should refrain from a hasty judgment that there was a danger of attack on the Tiwas by the Muslims in the Nellie area. The Nellie area is situated in the southern part of the Nagaon District, and Muslims are a minority here. Around Muladhari, there was a small pocket of about 10 villages inhabited by the Muslims but they were surrounded by villages inhabited by the Tiwas and the Kochs. When we consider this, the possibility of the Muslims attacking the Tiwas and the Assamese seem to be very low.

According to Spencer, such rumors circulate at the time of large-scale riots like the ones in Colombo in 1983 and in Delhi in 1984. Rumors circulate all the time, but at the time of large-scale violence people tend to believe certain representations as real and true, either in the absence of immediate empirical evidence or, in many cases, in direct contradiction to what they see around them (Spencer 2003: 1571–72). In the case of the Nellie incident too, the AASU activists and other villagers felt that the threat of attacks from the neighboring Muslim villages was acute and real. At the time of the violence, the area was tense due to the political disturbance caused by the forced election and its boycott. Even in rural areas like Nellie, the breakdown of law and order and threat of violence against civilian populations was palpable and imminent.

RIOTERS AND MORALITY: SELF-DEFENSE, RATHER THAN ECONOMIC DEPRIVATION

In any case, the villagers believed the rumor and took what they thought was *preemptive* action. They placed importance on the "fact" that there had been trouble between the Tiwas and the Muslims in a village 10–20 km away from them, and that was relevant to them. It should be noted that it was not land alienation which was emphasized as the main cause of the attack. People focused more on the danger of the attack from the Muslim side and cited it as the main reason for taking recourse to violence.

The tendency to cite self-defense as the primary motive for initiating violence during riots is not unique to the incident at Nellie. Spencer argued that in the case of the killing of the Tamils in 1983 and the anti-Sikh riots in Delhi in 1984, the rioters mentioned self-defense as a motive for the killings. He stated: "What the crowd was doing to Sikhs and Tamils was what the crowd believed Sikhs and Tamils were doing, or going to do, to them." (Spencer 2003: 1571). In addition to this perception of being at the receiving end, Horowitz also argued that rumors form an essential part of the riot process, and "they justify the violence that is about to occur (with their) severity (being) an indicator of the severity of the impending violence" (Horowitz 2001: 74–75).

In many of the discussions and conversations I had with the Tiwa, Koch, and Assamese respondents, the danger of attack (by the Muslims) was cited as more important and acute than that of land alienation. However, scholars and journalists who have done a postfacto analysis of the Assam movement have cited land alienation as one of the major factors leading to the violence (Kimura 2003: 233–34). This point will be discussed in the next chapter. The attackers and victims I interviewed suggested that the violence was the result of the aftermath of the elections. In addition, the attackers also cited kidnapping of girls, or purported attacks by the Muslims as "direct causes" for the violence.[19] "Structural causes" were of course not irrelevant to the killings, but what the rioters saw as a cause was usually more simple and prosaic.

In the Nellie area, at the time, threats against more vulnerable members, with the killing of children or kidnapping of girls, for example, had already taken place. Moreover, as shown in the statement, a clash between the Tiwas and the Muslims had also taken place in the northern part, and the villagers in the Nellie area were already involved. In this situation, there was certainly a group of people who seized the opportunity, trying to drive out the Muslims in order to gain access to their land. At the same time, there were local leaders who opposed the attack. During my interviews, several respondents told me that they opposed the movement or did not participate in the attack.

The presence of structural causes, such as the land issue, or of the motive to seize the opportunity to pursue an interest, were not strong enough to persuade those who opposed the attack. The villagers in the Nellie area participated in the attack under circumstances of an acute threat against them where they had no expectation of the police or security forces protecting them. What can be learned from the narratives of the Nellie massacre is that, in this case, self-defense emerged as the most important factor in decision making regarding the attack. In other words, at that time, the villagers' security in terms of life and property had already been threatened.

Antipathy towards the Congress government, which was already shared widely among the local people, could be counted as another important factor in the decision. Whether they supported the movement or not, the local people in the area recognized that the Congress would not protect them, as it sided with the Muslims. Distrust of the Congress government, which did not take any action towards those creating trouble, and the fact that the police and security forces did not (or could not) take any action to protect the locals, led people to decide to protect themselves. In this sense, the Nellie incident was an attempt by the local people to challenge the Congress regime and to try to protect their security and interests.

ROLE OF "OUTSIDERS" AND THE CONSTRUCTION OF COMMUNITY IN VIOLENCE

It is again through the circulation of rumor that the line between enemy and ally was created. For instance, respondents would say: "The Tiwas came to 'our' village;" or "The Muslims went to 'their' village." The line between "us" and "them" was being demarcated in the ritualistic narration of these incidents and this also led to the important marker of deciding who belonged to which community. In other words, the rumor remained an important process in the construction of community in the event of collective violence.

In the narrative, the advent of "outsiders" in Muladhari became the key factor in the decision to attack. According to views expressed in my interviews, the Muslims came from a village, Gorjan, where they had trouble with the Tiwas earlier. It is worth noting the difference between such statements and others that also attest to amicable and conflict-free relations between the Muslims and their attackers. Both the attackers and the victims endorse the latter view.[20]

Such narratives, which attribute the violence or the cause of the violence to "outsiders," are not unique to the attackers of the Nellie incident. Gyanendra Pandey pointed out that it was the way that face-to-face local communities[21] had to reconcile with disturbing memories of violence. He argued that nations deal with the moment of violence in their past by the relatively simple stratagem of drawing a neat boundary around themselves, distinguishing sharply between "us" and "them," and pronouncing the act of violence an act of the Other or an act necessitated by a threat to the self. The local communities, on the other hand, have to live with the memories of the violence more uncertainly, and continuously, than nations and states (Pandey 2001: 177). Thus, they attribute the violence or the cause of the violence to the outsiders.

Violence and Identity

Foreigners, Muslims, or Mymensinghia—Views of the Rioters

In the violence that took place during the election disturbance, the Muslims of East Bengal origin were perceived as the important "Other" who were seen as a threat to the local people. This happened in other parts of Assam as well. One question comes into play here: Did the movement leaders' claims that the foreigners were grabbing the land play any role in demarcating the community? In other words, were they taken to be "foreigners," as the movement leaders claimed? Or were they attacked simply because they were Muslims and not because they were "outsiders"? This is an important point to bear in mind when we analyze the character of the violence.

In the first place, if we look closely at the narratives of the Assamese and Tiwa villagers, they do not use the terms "foreigners" (*bideshi*) or "Muslims" (*Mussalmans*). Mostly, people in villages use the term *miya*s or *Mymensinghia*s. *Miya* is a term which refers to a Muslim and in the Assamese context specifically to those from East Bengal. *Mymensinghia* denotes people from Mymensingh District in erstwhile East Bengal, presently Bangladesh. The term indicates peasants hailing from the district, but it often happens that the term *miya* and *Mymensinghia* are used interchangeably.

In the course of my interviews, I noticed that the top student leaders used the term "foreigner" to denote the target of their political mobilization. However, local student leaders used the terms "minority" and "Muslim," while in rural areas such as Nellie, people often used the term *miya*s or *Mymensinghia*s. It is important to see from the transformation of the terms how the local leaders—usually located in the smaller towns—as well as the villagers in the rural areas interpreted the movement and the violence.

In the beginning, the AASU engaged in a Gandhian-style nonviolent movement. However, the movement leaders did not take any action to prevent incidents of harassment against the Muslims being mistaken as "Bangladeshis." There was a group attack in the northern part of Kamrup District in 1980. There was a gap between the movement's official slogan and the incidents taking place on the ground, yet instead of taking preventive measures, the movement leaders utilized anti-Muslim sentiments to mobilize the masses to join the movement. Some Assamese intellectuals have pointed to this to argue that the AASU took a secular claim to garner support from outside the state, but in fact took a xenophobic attitude inside Assam (Gohain 1985: 20).

The student leader who gave me the account of the decision-making process in the attack used the term "Muslim" as did most other local leaders. However, a village elder explained the incident in this way:

> It was not a clash between Hindus and Muslims, but it was targeted against *miyas*. *Miyas* are immigrants who came from Bangladesh. The movement aimed to deport *bideshis* [foreigners]. Thus it was targeted against *miyas*, particularly *Mymensinghias*.[22]

It is important to note that in his narrative, the term *bideshi* was used almost as an equivalent to *miya* and *Mymensinghia*. It is not that the Assamese and Tiwa villagers are ignorant of the fact that most Muslims in the villages that were attacked came to Assam in the colonial period. However, because of their East Bengal origin, they are often perceived or mistaken to be Bangladeshis. Thus, when the boycott took place during the State Legislative Assembly election, an atmosphere whereby the Muslims were regarded as "Bangladeshis" already existed, and any harassment or violence against them was socially tolerated under the ideology of the anti-foreigner movement. Rumors of foreigners hiding in Muslim villages added to people's suspicions, and contributed to their tendency to target all the Muslims of immigrant origin as the "enemy." In this way, the notion of foreigners was slowly attributed to the Muslims of East Bengal origin. Thus, the movement leaders' identification of foreigners as targets of their ire, were interpreted to mean anti–Bengali-Muslim peasants in the local context, by the middle class urban Assamese and their rural counterparts. The attacks however took place in the rural areas since most Muslims with origins in East Bengal were located there.

Muslims as the "Important Other" in Assam: Citizenship and Religion in India

The Nellie incident had a tremendous impact on Hindu–Muslim relations in Assam. Until then, it has been said, the state was relatively free from communal tension. Except for the disturbance in the lower Assam districts in 1950, which occurred in relation to the Partition and the violence that took place in East Pakistan at the time, it was rare that the Muslims of East Bengal origin were targeted in episodes of collective violence. Indeed, during the 1960s and the 1970s when the language movement was prominent in the state, it was always the middle-class Bengalis (mostly Hindus) who were targeted and defined as a "threat" by the middle-class Assamese. The Muslim peasants who declared their mother tongue to be Assamese were not targeted till the antiforeigner movement started in the late 1970s.

It should be noted that at the time numerous violent incidents took place during the election period, and the targets were not only the Muslims of East

Bengal origin. In other incidents, the Bengali Hindus, the Nepalis, and the Biharis were also attacked. In the Gohpur incident, another indigenous tribal group, the Bodos, attacked the Assamese. Thus, there was local variation in the identity of the victims.

On the other hand, when one considers the death count, one sees that most victims were the Muslims of East Bengal origin (Baruah 1999: 132). This is also a prominent feature of communal violence in other parts of India. Whenever anti-Pakistan or anti-Bangladesh sentiments arise, the Muslims are targeted even though they are genuine citizens born in India. The Muslims are always suspected of their loyalty to the country. Such notions are deeply embedded in the history of Partition and nation-state formation in India and Pakistan (and Bangladesh). In that sense, although the antiforeigner movement was not explicitly against the Muslims, the issue of citizenship tended to be connected to the issue of religion, particularly against the Muslims.

After the Nellie incident, those Muslims who were earlier active participants or eager supporters of the movement withdrew their support. Many active workers in the AASU stopped participating in blockades and demonstrations. This was not only among the Muslims of immigrant origin, but also with the Muslim communities who had settled before colonization and were seen as "indigenous" in Assamese society. One of the top student leaders from the indigenous community resigned from his position after the incident. People reacted differently to the Nellie incident,[23] but in any case it left a scar in Assamese society, which until then was believed to be relatively free from communal tension.

As mentioned in this chapter, the Muslims became the important "Other" after the antiforeigner movement. Whenever the slogan against "foreigners" arises, the Muslim community fears deportation. There have been many cases where the Muslim immigrants were suspected of being illegal immigrants and have had to produce documents in order to prove their place of birth.[24] In later years, the antiforeigner movement has been influenced by the rise of pan-Indian Hindu nationalism and the Bharatiya Janata Party brand of politics. Hindutva did not change the politics of Assam, but it took advantage of the Assamese fear of the Muslims and was thus partly successful in gaining some organizational basis in Assam.

We thus see that the issue of citizenship transformed into violence against the Muslims in the Nellie incident in Assam in 1983. Although the leaders claimed that it was the foreigners who should be deported, when the violence began the victims were the descendants of the ordinary immigrant Muslims.

Conclusion

The analysis in this chapter reveals that in the narratives of the riot participants, the perception of threat from the Muslims as felt by the villagers was crucial when they made their decision to attack. From their perspective, it was not ideology or land alienation but the more acute and directly felt threat which made them attack their Muslim neighbors.

This does not mean that the ideology of the antiforeigner movement or land alienation was irrelevant to the event. On the contrary, it was relevant in the sense that they were the important factors in demarcating the "Other" when the violence took place. What should be noted here is that it is misleading to assume that local people were puppets of ideology and structural causes. Instead, they interpreted these factors from their own perspectives and took a decision to protect themselves.

Without argument, it can be said that the degree of such agency of the rioters may vary in each case. In rural areas where the village-level community and its hierarchies are strong, the impact of external factors is limited. The scenario may be different in urban areas, where riots most frequently occur in India.

In this chapter, I have tried to show how ordinary people took the decision to attack their neighbors at a time of extreme political crisis. The villagers were not totally controlled by the movement leaders or communal forces, but they still chose to riot. Although the scale of the incident was large, the villages around Nellie were not extraordinary in any sense. It could have happened in any village in Assam. In order to understand this, we need to listen to the complicated, and sometimes competing, narratives and the fragmented accounts of the villagers more carefully.

Notes

1. According to the *District Gazetteer of Assam*, the Tiwa (called Lalungs at the time) population of the district was 28,985 in the 1901 census. Because of the *kala azar*, an epidemic, the population diminished significantly between 1891 and 1901, declining in number from 46,658 to 28,958 (*District Gazetteer of Assam, Nowgong* 1905: 81–82).

2. The Line System was an administrative measure to divide the areas inhabited by the immigrants and the local populations. It was introduced by the officials of Nagaon District in order to prevent any friction over occupation of land between the immigrants and the local populations.

3. Maps of the area are available in *Report of the Special Officer Appointed for the Examination of the Professional Grazing Reserves in the Assam Valley* (1944). For a discussion on the PGR, see Guha (1977: 281, 284–85).

4. There still are Tiwa people living in the hill areas in Karbi Anglong District, which is adjacent to present-day Morigaon and Nagaon Districts.

5. According to Baruah, most peasants in Assam conducted shifting cultivation. He argued that in the context of precolonial Assam, it was not only the "tribals" who conducted shifting cultivation, and to draw the line of "primitive" and "civilized" between shifting and settled cultivation did not have any foundation in the reality of agricultural practices in Assam (Baruah 2005: 89).

6. The Assam Land and Revenue Regulation 1886, Chapter X, passed in 1947.

7. Village unit adopted for administration and survey.

8. Group interview with villagers in Koraiguri village, November 15, 2001.

9. Group interview with villagers in Merua Gaon. November 24, 2001.

10. Group interview with villagers in Koraiguri village, November 15, 2001.

11. Group interview with villagers in Koraiguri village, November 15, 2001.

12. Interview with a former AAGSP activist in Amlighat village, November 11, 2001.

13. Interview with a former AAGSP activist in Parahguri village, November 12, 2001.

14. "Doubtful voters" or "D-voters" are people whose citizenships are not confirmed or are suspected as illegal migrants. Once they are listed as doubtful voters, their right to vote is suspended until legal examination. But in practice, the process is arbitrary and becomes a measure to harass mainly the Muslims of immigrant origin and the Nepalis, who are often suspected as illegal migrants.

15. Group interview with villagers in Koraiguri village, November 15, 2001.

16. Personal interview with a former leader of Lalung organization, February 15, 2002.

17. Personal interview with a schoolteacher in a village just north of Nellie area, November 24, 2001. All subsequent narratives in this section are from this interview.

18. "Lalung" is the old, pejorative name ascribed to the Tiwas. The memorandum was submitted to the prime minister of India on June 24, 1983 by Lalung Darbar, a sociocultural organization of the Tiwas. The organization first submitted a memorandum on the demand for the autonomous district of the Tiwas in 1967. I thank Hemendra Narayan for sending me the document on my request.

19. I thank Professor Virginius Xaxa for pointing out the difference between direct causes and structural causes in this analysis.

20. On this point, see the arguments in Kimura (2003).
21. Rural communities where people can recognize each other by face.
22. Personal interview with a villager in Tetelia Tribal Block, November 15, 2001.
23. On the different responses to the Nellie incident among the Muslims see Saikia (2004: 66–67).
24. Interview with Muslim residents of East Bengal descent in Lahorighat, February 2007.

6

Memories of the Massacre*

Memory and Violence

In this chapter, I focus on how the collective memory of violence is formed in different communities and how the process is essential in the formation of the groups' collective identities. The foci of the chapter are the Tiwas (the main group which participated in the Nellie massacre) as well as the Muslims of immigrant origin, the survivors of the incident. Although both the groups are minorities in Assamese society, if we compare them, their identity formation and articulation after the antiforeigner movement were quite different. At the time of the research in 2001–2002, the Tiwa movement for autonomy was quite active and they were trying to develop a distinct identity from the mainstream Assamese community, while the Muslims were silent and their narratives were fragmented.

Compared to the established nations that have already developed their official national history, minority groups (so-called ethnic, religious, or linguistic minorities or tribes) in sovereign states have to choose whether or not to articulate their collective identities. Although recently there has been increasing evidence of minority groups becoming politically aware and engaging in organized movements, there are still groups that do not (or cannot) choose to claim their rights as a specific group, and thus assimilate into the dominant nation. When a minority group chooses to distinguish itself from the dominant nation and tries to establish its own identity, it needs to narrate its own history and define itself as a subject. On the other hand, if its members choose to assimilate, they do not need their own version of history. In the 1983 Nellie massacre, the Tiwas, the group generally

* An earlier version of this chapter appeared as "Memories of the Massacre: Violence and the Collective Identity in the Narratives on the Nellie Incident" in *Asian Ethnicity*, Vol. 4. No. 2, published by Taylor and Francis on June 1, 2003.

recognized as the attacker was active in developing its own version of the violence, while the Muslims, the group seen as the victim was not. In this massacre, the interrelationships of the groups were complex. This is because both the attackers—the Tiwas, an indigenous community in Assam—and the survivors, primarily comprising the Muslims of immigrant origin from the East Bengal region (present-day Bangladesh) were subordinate groups in Assamese society economically, politically, and socially. Here, we can see the way in which minorities establish their own versions of narratives against the master narrative of the dominant group, and the way in which the minority group distances itself from the latter.

I am going to compare the narratives of the Tiwas (attackers), the Muslims of immigrant origin (survivors) and the movement leaders (a dominant group of Hindu Assamese) which I collected in my research trip to the Nellie area in November 2001 and February 2002. My central argument is that each group has their own interpretation of the cause of the incident, and in the process of recalling the past, they select "facts" from their memories. By looking at the narration of the violence, the power relations between the groups become clear. At the same time, through the experience of violence, the power relations are reconstructed and the boundaries between the communities are redefined. It is my argument that the decision taken by the minority groups—whether to establish their own history or not—is deeply related to their political choice available to them: demand for autonomy or forced to assimilate into the dominant community.

Memories of the Massacre: Method and Locations

During my fieldwork in Nellie, I was fortunate enough to interview both the attackers and the survivors, which is very rare in the study of communal violence in contemporary India. Especially in urban areas (where most of the collective violence take place), there is a difficulty in specifying who the attackers were. Even though the attackers can be specified, it would be dif-ficult to ask them about the participation in the attack, as they would deny the involvement in it. On the other hand, regarding the survivors, in many cases they are displaced from their residence at the time of the attack and it is often difficult to locate them. In the case of the Nellie massacre, however, both the survivors and the attackers could go back to their villages and continue to live—though not in complete harmony—with their neighbors again. My fieldwork was conducted nearly 20 years after the incident and thus the issue ceased to be sensitive in the area.

Of course, there were some difficulties and limits in doing fieldwork in the area affected by large-scale collective violence. In my first research in 2001, I had taken an Assamese Hindu or Tiwa interpreter in the area. Because of their identities, the Muslims hesitated to give their comments on the incident. A few times, we were told to go to different places or asked, "Why do you want to know about that, it's finished. We live in peace now." This is in sharp contrast with my follow-up interviews in 2007, where people kept talking of their loss and agony to my Muslim (of immigrant origin) research partner. The experience of the research in 2007 will be supplemented in the concluding chapter.

In fieldwork conducted in 2001, compared to the survivors, the attackers were more vocal in telling their stories. There were a few people who admitted that they joined the attack and killed, and most of the villagers did not deny the fact that the villages on the north bank of the Kopili River lent their hands, *gheraoed*[1] the riverbank, and cut the way for escape. More importantly, they were very vocal in telling me why they did join the attack.

The argument in this chapter is based on interviews in two Muslim immigrant villages and two Tiwa villages. In each village, the number of persons interviewed was 10 to 15. I usually began by meeting a teacher or some key person with higher education in the village, followed by interviews with a few individuals, and then conducted group interviews with the villagers. No sampling was taken in the research, for it is difficult to stay in a village for a long time in order to study a violent incident.[2] Also, owing to my lack of proficiency in the Assamese language, I had to rely on the help of interpreters. However, by explaining the purpose of the research to the interpreters, and also by repeatedly asking questions myself to the interviewees, I was successful in grasping a basic idea of their views on the cause of the movement and ways of defining the "Other."

In these interviews, I focused on people's opinions rather than finding out "facts," such as, what happened on that day, who were the leaders of the attack, who mobilized the people, and who actually killed the victims. Instead, my focus was on the way people recognize what had happened and what they believe to be the cause of the incident. This line of inquiry is more important than fact-finding per se for the purpose of this study, because my focus is on narratives—the way people interpret the past according to their understanding of the present and the way they define the "Other." Therefore, my interview schedule consisted of only a few questions, so as to allow my respondents to talk as freely as possible.

The interviews were conducted in three main parts—the Muslim immigrant villages, the Tiwa villages, and the town of Morigaon. The Muslim villages were the actual site of the massacre. They are situated north of National Highway 37, and the village called Nellie is located beside the highway. As a relief camp for the victims of the massacre was set up in Nellie, the incident took its name from this village, but the actual site was 10–20 km away (Map 6.1).

Map 6.1
Sites of the Nellie Massacre

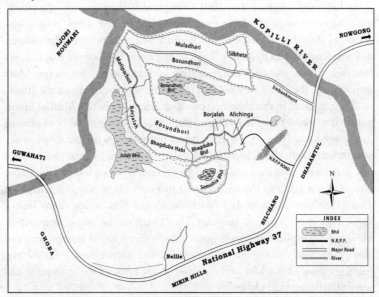

Source: Assam Freedom Fighters' Association, 1985.

Interviews were conducted in villages A and B in the Muslim immigrant area, and villages C and D in the Tetelia Tribal Block. Villages A and B are similar in their basic features. Most villagers engage in agriculture, and the main produce is rice. There is one lower primary school and one middle school (English medium) in each village, but there are no hospitals or health centers, and no drinking water or telephone facilities. Compared to these Muslim immigrant villages, the Tiwa villages are in a slightly better condition, especially in terms of the maintenance of schools and the number of teachers per student (higher since there are fewer students), but there are no significant differences between them. The situation of village C is similar to that of villages A and B. Here too, the main produce of the villagers is rice and there is only one lower primary school. Village D has the best facilities of these four villages. It has three lower primary schools, one middle school, and a health center. Also, there is one high school in a nearby village.

It should be noted here that in village C, the influence of the All Tiwa Students' Union (ATSU) has been quite strong. This body was established in 1989 after the antiforeigner movement. Several active members of the ATSU and other closely related organizations such as the All Tiwa Women's Association are residents of the village.

On the whole, the Tiwa villages are in better condition than the Muslim immigrant villages. In terms of land possession and family size, the Tiwa villagers own larger areas of land and have smaller family than the Muslims. In terms of education, although the number of schools is similar, the proportion of children attending is very different. In the Muslim immigrant villages, people tend to have many children and there are fewer chances for them to get an education. However, in this locality, it can be said that the standard of living of the Tiwas and the Muslim immigrants is almost equal, though the Tiwas have slightly better access to education.

Narratives on the Nellie Massacre

Different Narratives on the Cause of the Massacre: The Muslims, the Tiwas, and the Local Movement Leaders

In the interviews,[3] I started asking the details of the incident. Contrary to my expectations, the explanations about the sequence of events relating to the massacre that were given by the Muslims, the Tiwas, and the local movement leaders were quite consonant with one another. The emphasis and some of the details such as the timing and the grouping of the attackers differed from each other but, generally, their explanations were not contradictory, and it is possible to find common factors and descriptions of the sequence of events. However, opinions on the cause of the massacre were widely different.

Broadly speaking, the narrations of the three groups of people— the Muslims, the Tiwas, and the local movement leaders—as to the cause of the violence were different. Although individual views on the cause of the massacre differed in many ways from person to person, we find common characteristics in each group.

THE MUSLIMS: REVENGE FOR PARTICIPATION IN THE ELECTION

According to the Muslims, the massacre was a revenge for their participation in the election. At that time, the All Assam Students' Union (AASU) and the All Assam Gana Sangram Parishad (AAGSP) had called for a boycott of the election. However, some of the Muslims went to the election booth and tried to cast their ballots. Most of those interviewed considered this to be a cause of the massacre.

For example, when asked about the cause of the incident, villagers in village A explained it in this way:

> The election was to be held. And the people of Assam under the banner of AASU decided. They decided not to get involved in the election process. So they asked all [of] us people not to vote. They threatened. But some 15–16 people went to Alichinga polling centre. They went there for voting but they found nobody there, no polling officers, no election authority people. And they got back.[4]

Also in village B, one villager explained the cause of the massacre as follows:

> Some students union told [us] not to cast votes.... No óne was going to vote on that election, only from Nellie a few...6–7 people went to vote. No election officer came.... Their main demand was not to cast votes. [But] a few went to cast their vote [and] revenge was taken against us.[5]

From these statements, it is obvious that the villagers view the massacre basically as a revenge for their participation in the election. Also, when asked about the confrontation with the local people, all of them replied that, before the movement started, there was no trouble between them and the local people, such as the Tiwas and the Assamese.

THE TIWAS: THE LEADERSHIP OF THE AASU

The Tiwas' views were more diverse than that of the Muslim immigrants. In village C, the incidents of the kidnapping of girls by the immigrants were cited as the cause of the incident, as noted in Chapter 5. According to them,

> They [the Muslims] used to take girls and they used to keep them at their homes. We were very much offended, and this thing was shared by the AASU and the Assamese people.[6]

However, in another Tiwa village, village D, the people interviewed did not refer to the kidnapping of girls as a cause of the massacre. Although they admitted that such kinds of incidents did occur, they did not mention this matter until they were asked about it. Rather, they claimed that the election and the movement were the direct causes.

> The main issue was that particular movement. We only knew that antiforeigner movement is going on and led by the AASU. We felt one crisis [of foreigners' influx] is going on with the Assamese people, so we united and we gave a stand.[7]

Interestingly, when asked whether they had any trouble with the Muslim immigrants, most of them said that there had been no trouble and that they had a good relationship with them. Even in village C, where the people complained vociferously about the kidnapping of girls, they reported that these things did not start happening until the early 1980s. Before that—that is before the movement—they had no trouble with the immigrants.

Also, although their views on the cause of the massacre appeared to vary, there was one striking similarity in the description of the incident. It was that the AASU and the AAGSP, and not the villagers, took on the leadership of the massacre. It was quite strong in village C. A villager who participated in the activities of the AASU at the time said,

> It was led by the AASU. But they cheated.[8]

Also, in village D, after the interview was over and the tape recorder was switched off, the people started talking about their mistrust of the movement leaders.

> We were misguided. We helped the Assamese, but once it came to light they did not take the responsibility and criticized the Tiwas. They said, "These

people are wild." Many people started the violence. Not the Tiwas. But they did not take responsibility and escaped.[9]

As is clear from this statement, their emphasis is that the AASU and the AAGSP did not take responsibility for the massacre, but instead laid the blame on the Tiwas. Although they did not deny that most of the villagers participated in the massacre, they believed that their role was merely to offer help because the movement leaders had asked for it. Therefore, even if the people in village C claimed that there was trouble regarding the kidnapping of girls, this was just the secondary reason for their participation in the massacre. They suggested that the AASU used this matter to gain support to attack the immigrants.

THE LOCAL MOVEMENT LEADERS: TROUBLES BETWEEN THE LOCAL PEOPLE AND THE MUSLIMS

The members of the AASU and the AAGSP were the most vocal and clear in explaining the cause of the massacre. Most of them claimed that confrontation had arisen between the local people and the Muslims on various issues such as land alienation and cultural identity. It was the continued influx of the immigrants from the East Bengal region that gave rise to this confrontation. For example, Mr X, a member of the AAGSP stated:

> Some mistrust between the two communities...immigrant Muslims and local people. Mainly tribal people...the Tiwas and the Karbis and also the Assamese communities. They [are] gradually grabbing the land. The crisis of identity. Local people feel that they [have] become minority. Actually religious minority [have] become majority in that area.... Direct cause is identity. The identity of indigenous people.[10]

Mr Y, who was a convener of the AAGSP in Morigaon, narrated it in more detail. He emphasized that the Muslim immigrants harassed the local people, forcing them to move from their homes.

> The thing is this, if Muslim people are inhabited near the Assamese villages, generally, paddy field is forcefully harvested by the Muslim people at night. And for such type of misbehavior of the Muslim people, the Assamese people generally think that they are harassed by the Muslim people.... In that way, they are stealing their cattle, stealing the Hindu girls, in that way they are harassing the Assamese people and lastly, it happens that the Assamese people

[were forced to] sell the land to the Muslim people.... In that way, the Muslim people were grabbing the land of the Assamese people.[11]

To the local movement leaders, it was clearly the appropriation of their land that caused the massacre. From their point of view, the cause was long standing, with mistrust between the local people and the Muslims of immigrant origin deepening day by day. Moreover, when asked about the relation of the AASU and the AAGSP to the massacre, all of them denied that the AASU and the AAGSP had any role in it.

It is possible to summarize the pattern of the narratives as follows. To the Muslims, the massacre was seen as revenge for their participation in the election. The Tiwas, on the other hand, emphasized that the AASU and the AAGSP had urged them to attack the Muslims, though they also had their own reasons for attacking the Muslims, since they had troubles regarding the security of their members. And the local movement leaders considered the massacre to have been an outcome of the continued influx of the Muslims and their expropriation of land.

Taking a look at the three styles of the narratives on the cause of the massacre, it can be said that each developed their own version and selectively picked up the "facts" from their memories according to what they considered suitable for their stories. However, the extent of acceptance of the narratives is not the same. Some narratives are more widely known and accepted in society, while others are subordinate. In the next section, I shall argue that the local movement leaders' narrative is dominant and others are subordinate in Assamese society; and I suggest the reason for it.

The Dominant Narrative in Society: Land Alienation by Immigrants

In the writings of academics and journalists in Assam and the rest of India, the problem of land alienation by the Muslims of Bengali origin has up to now been regarded as the cause of the Nellie massacre. The indigenous peoples in Assam resented losing their land because of the continued Muslim influx. And when scholars and journalists try to analyze the cause of the Nellie massacre, they often suggest that the Tiwas were deeply resentful of land alienation. We have already seen that the pan-Indian media, the *Indian Express* in particular, reported the cause of the incident as tribal land alienation immediately after the incident took place. It seems that this interpretation is largely accepted by scholars and journalists from Assam. For example, Sanjib Baruah wrote,

> Some of the worst violence occurred in villages around Nellie, an area where the Tiwa people once had their kingdom; much of the area is now settled by Bengali immigrants and their descendants. Tiwas (also called Lalungs) are a "plains tribe" who had lost much of their land to immigrants from East Bengal. (Baruah 1999: 134)

Similarly, the Assamese journalist Sanjoy Hazarika wrote,

> In the case of Nellie and its surrounding villages, those who sold their lands were the Tiwas. Their bitterness grew as they saw the immigrants nourish the soil and grow more crops, making profits on fields which were, until recently, their own.... Perhaps it [the day of the massacre] would be better described as pay-back day. (Hazarika 2001: 46)

It is clear that the cause of the massacre given in these two writings is consistent with that of the local movement leaders. It should be noted that most of the local movement leaders in Morigaon were college lecturers or schoolteachers, and so-called caste-Hindu Assamese. Being intellectuals, they had better access to the top movement leaders' claims and newspaper reports. It can be said that the local movement leaders' narrative represents the dominant narrative of the Assamese intellectuals.

Although the Muslims, the Tiwas, and the local movement leaders talk about the "cause" of one incident, the dimensions of their narratives are different. The local movement leaders state the structural cause, while the Muslim immigrants and the Tiwas talk about the immediate cause. The Muslims of immigrant origin trace the cause to their participation in the election. They recognize the violence only as a solitary event, and do not relate it to the history of continued immigration or the movement. Thus, they suggest only the "direct" cause of the incident. As for the Tiwas, when they talk about the "cause," their statement also refers to the immediate cause, the kidnapping of the female members of their community and the AASU's leadership.

However, the movement leaders narrate the cause in a totally different way. They attribute the cause of the violence to the historical problem of land alienation among the local people, especially the Tiwas, by the immigrants.

They argue that immigration itself is a fundamental problem and suggest that the cause of the problem lies in the social structure of Assamese society. Unlike the Tiwas and the Muslim immigrants, they make no reference to any direct cause.

There might be several factors accounting for the difference in the interpretations. However, it should be noticed that the narratives of the attackers and the survivors—people who actually participated in and were affected by the massacre—became subordinate, while that of the local movement leaders, which represent the opinions and viewpoints of Assamese intellectuals, are dominant in Assamese society.

Exercising Agency and Establishing Collective Identity in Counter-Narratives

So far, we have seen that there are three styles of narratives on the cause of the massacre, and among the three, the local movement leaders' narrative is the dominant one in Assamese society. In this version, the Muslims of Bengali origin are projected as the "enemy" who harassed local people and forced them to leave the place. Thus, they suggest that although the local people are the attackers in the violence, they are actually the victims of the Muslims' misbehavior. In this style of narrative, the Muslims of immigrant origin are positioned as the "Other" and the local people, including the Assamese and the indigenous communities, are lumped into one category distinct from the immigrants.

However, even though the Tiwas supported the AASU and the antiforeigner movement, and participated in the massacre, later they distanced themselves from the Assamese and sought to develop/establish their own identity. On the other hand, the Muslim immigrants did not choose to define clearly the Tiwas or the AASU as the "Other." Here, I analyze the reason behind the difference.

Defining the "Other": Identity in Counter-Narratives

As noted in the Introduction, by examining the people's narratives of the experience of the violence, it is possible to see their definition of the "Other."

In this process, they construct the boundary between "we" and "they." However, in the case of the Muslims, although they stressed the gravity of the sufferings they experienced, they refrained from identifying the attackers. When asked who the attackers were, some of the people replied that they did not know, while others vaguely defined them as "local people."

As shown in the previous section, to the Muslims of immigrant origin, it was the members of the AASU who took revenge on them because some of the Muslim peasants had gone to cast their votes. However, they stopped short of defining the AASU as a complete "enemy." When asked what they thought about the movement, they acknowledged that the movement itself was right. At the same time, they were quick to point out that the movement leaders harassed the immigrants who had been living in Assam before the partition and independence of India. Their main criticism was on this point. Therefore, the point of the argument was on the misidentification of the foreigners and not on the movement policy itself.

It can be said that as there have been serious controversies over the legitimacy of the immigrants' existence in Assam, criticism of the movement policy itself could be a dangerous act for the Muslims. When they expressed their criticism, they were often regarded as illegal foreigners. The movement leaders often used the logic that "if you are Assamese, you should support our policy." Therefore, this made it difficult for them to criticize the movement policy itself, or to distinguish themselves from the "Assamese." Being Muslims of Bengal origin, they are prone to be regarded as "foreigners." If they make a move for distinct identity apart from the Assamese, there is a possibility that their existence in Assam would be threatened.

Thus, in a way, they are forced to assimilate with the mainstream Assamese. They lack political base for they are Muslims; at the same time, they suffer the disadvantage of being Muslims, a religious minority in the state. For these two reasons, they are not able to choose and distinguish themselves from the Assamese people. It was especially prominent in 2001–2002, right after the Asom Gana Parishad (AGP) had ruled the state for five years from 1996 to 2001.

The Tiwas were more successful than the Muslims in defining the "Other" and developing themselves as a subject. The Tiwas' narrative is the most interesting in this case because, although their "enemy" at the time of the massacre was the Muslims, in the narrative they differentiate themselves both from the movement leaders and the mainstream Assamese. One Tiwa woman, a member of the All Tiwa Women's Association, observed,

Before the massacre, there was no difference among the Tiwas and the Rabhas [another plains tribe in this area]. We were all tribes as well as Assamese. However, though the AASU said, "We are all Assamese," they cheated us. They had slogans like "come out of your home." We participated in the movement because [we thought] when they become government they will do the development properly but they did not. The AGP came into power in 1985. The All Tiwa Students' Union was formed in 1989. The situation is [the] same for the Rabhas or Plain Karbis. They [were] disappointed [with] the AGP and the AASU so they formed their own organizations.[12]

In this statement, the AASU, the AGP and the Assamese community as a whole are criticized for betraying the expectations of the Tiwas and for failing to attend to the economic development of the people. It can be seen that the speaker not only questions the issue of the leadership in the massacre, but also raises the economic backwardness and neglected status of the Tiwas in Assam politics. In this context, the Nellie incident is regarded as one strong evidence which shows the disregard of the Tiwas by the mainstream Assamese.

Autonomy or Assimilation? Choice of Strategy and Identity by Minorities

Although their narratives are equally subordinate in Assamese society, the degree of success in developing themselves as a subject in their own history differs widely in the case of the Tiwas and the Muslims. As documented in the previous section, the Tiwas are quite successful and positive in distinguishing their identity from the Assamese, while the Muslims are not. It is my argument that the reason for the difference lies in the Muslims' present status in Assam politics and their distance from the Assamese. At this point, even though it is difficult to prove with concrete evidence, I would suggest the probability of a relationship between the development of memories of violence and collective identity.

It has often been argued that the indigenous peoples in the plains areas like the Tiwas had slowly adopted the Assamese way of life and the language, and that they were in a process of assimilation (Guha 1984: 59; Hussain 1993: 171). However, from the late 1980s, a section of the Tiwa people started to assert their own identity.

The Tiwa movements were not totally absent prior to the 1980s. Indeed, as early as 1967, they had established the Lalung Darbar, a socioeconomic and cultural organization which demanded the creation of a separate autonomous district for the Lalung people under the Sixth Schedule[13] of the Constitution of India. The main purpose for demanding an autonomous district at the time was to promote the economic development of the Tiwa people.[14]

To intensify the demand and realize this objective, the All Tiwa Students' Union was formed in 1989 and, together with the Lalung Darbar, they demanded the establishment of the Autonomous Tiwa District. In 1994, an ordinance of the governor of Assam created the Lalung Autonomous Council (LAC). At that time, the Congress was the ruling party in the state, and the LAC was established under the leadership of Chief Minister Hiteswar Saikia.[15]

However, the LAC did not meet the demands put up by the Tiwas. The main demand of the Autonomous Lalung District Demand Committee (an offshoot of the Lalung Darbar and some other Lalung organizations) was the extension of the Sixth Schedule provisions and hence the creation of the autonomous district with a distinct territory. But this demand was not fulfilled.

Also, according to the ordinance of the governor of Assam in 1994, 26 out of 30 members of the general council of the LAC were elected directly by the state government. Therefore, when the ruling party of the state government changed, the members of the general council too would be reelected.

Because of the inadequacy of the LAC, some people termed it a puppet organization of the state government and continued their demand for an Autonomous District Council. This led to the creation of the Autonomy Demand Struggling Forum (ADSF) in 1994. To strengthen their demand, a political wing, the United People's Front (UPF), was formed under the ADSF, which contested the election to the State Legislative Assembly. The ADSF is an organization constituted mainly of the Tiwas, but the UPF includes other tribal communities such as the Rabhas and the Plain Karbis as well. At the time of the research in 2001–2002, the ATSU maintained a strong relationship with the ADSF and was a part of the UPF, as well as of the students' unions of the Rabhas and the Plain Karbis.[16]

The Tiwa autonomous movement is not only political and economic in nature, but also has a cultural aspect. The Tiwa Sahitya Sabha, the Tiwa literary organization that was formed in 1981, has a strong relationship with this movement. Initially, the Tiwa Sahitya Sabha did not have any political links, but in 1993, Tulsi Bordoloi, the present chairman of the ADSF, became the president of the Sabha. Also, after this period, the Tiwa Sahitya Sabha started using the Roman script instead of the Assamese script used earlier. In 1995, the Sabha published *Tiwa Matbadi*, a Tiwa–Assamese–English Dictionary, based on the Roman script. It can be said that the Tiwa Sahitya Sabha is moving towards establishing its own language and literature, differentiating itself from the language of the dominant group (Kholar 1995).[17]

The discourse which lamented the betrayal of the AASU and the AAGSP is particularly strong in the area where the ATSU and the ADSF are active. There has been a process of reinterpretation of the Nellie incident when the ATSU and the ADSF assert the Tiwa collective identity. As analyzed in Chapter 5, in the decision-making process of the attack, the Tiwa villagers, together with the Kochs, the Hiras and other low-caste or indigenous communities, had exercised their agency and decided to attack the Muslims from a different perspective of the movement leaders and middle-class Assamese.

However, after the incident, when the responsibility of the attack was largely attributed to them, and when the caste-Hindu Assamese-centric policies became clear in the Assam Accord, the Tiwas took a different path from the Assamese. They also differentiated themselves from their Hindu neighbors (the Kochs and the Hiras) and exercised their agency through a movement for autonomy and assertion of the Tiwa identity. In this process, the memories of the Nellie massacre were utilized.

Compared to the active movement among the Tiwas, the Muslims of immigrant origin have been less articulate in establishing themselves as a distinct ethnic group in Assamese society. It has been pointed out that the Muslim peasants who have their origins in the Bengal region adopted the Assamese language and reported the same as their mother tongue in the census enumeration. Indeed, it was the Muslim peasants' adoption of Assamese language that made Assamese the majority language in the state of Assam (Dasgupta 2000: 15–19; Guha 1984: 59). Commenting on the development, Myron Weiner, the first foreign scholar to study the immigration problem in Assam before the antiforeigner movement was started by the AASU, pointed to an "unspoken coalition between the Assamese and the Bengali Muslims against the Bengali Hindus" (Weiner 1983: 284–85).

This situation has continued to the present. In 2002, the Asam Sahitya Sabha (ASS), the largest literary and cultural organization of the Assamese people, held its annual session in Kalgachia in Barpeta District. Kalgachia is an area dominated by the Muslims of immigrant origin. It was the first time in the history of the ASS that the session had taken place in such an area, and the Muslim people in Kalgachia largely welcomed it (*The Assam Tribune*, February 13, 2002).

There has been a significant change in the ASS's stance towards linguistic minorities in Assam. In the 1960s and in the 1970s, the ASS was the most influential organization that encouraged the introduction of Assamese as the official language in the state and the medium of instruction in schools. At the time, ASS was strongly criticized for imposing Assamese on indigenous communities and other non-Assamese speaking people. In the antiforeigner movement, the ASS was one of the core organizations that formed the AAGSP. However, in 2001, Homen Borgohain became ASS's president, and he adopted the policy of building a greater Assamese nationality. His concept of a greater Assamese nationality does not exclude people whose mother tongue is not Assamese. His view was inclusive in nature, emphasizing that those who work to promote Assamese literature and show an interest in Assamese language and literature should be accepted as Assamese people (Borgohain 2001; *The Assam Tribune*, February 13, 2002).

While the Muslim people in Kalgachia seemed to welcome this move, the Tiwas were still doubtful about this change in the ASS's stance. To my query whether the ASS was changing their stance, Tulsi Bordoloi, chairman of the ADSF and a former president of the Tiwa Sahitya Sabha, replied as follows:

> Yes, it is ah…. Actually, some measure has been taken by the ASS in case of development of language or the culture of the ethnic people. They have also taken the Muslim people [who] migrated to Assam, [and] given [them] the name "new Assamese." But it is not sufficient. How much damage had been already made, especially in case of ethnic people. In comparison to that, [the] measures taken by the ASS is not sufficient…. Many times, this Sahitya Sabha has been used as the platform of ethnic chauvinism. [This is a] mistake. If the ASS would have contributed to the development of Assamese language, ethnic culture, then there would not be any ethnic Sahitya Sabha.[18]

From the above argument, it can be said that the situation of the Tiwas and the Muslims of immigrant origin are very different. The Tiwas started seeking their own identity separate from the Assamese, and the Muslims of immigrant origin continued the same practice of linguistic assimilation to the Assamese. It is clear that the difference in the narratives of the Tiwas and the Muslim immigrants is related to their present political status, whether or not they can seek for a distinct identity. The Tiwas' political advantage helped them to differentiate themselves from the Assamese, while the Muslims are ambiguous on this point. What we see here is that people select "facts" from their memories and create their own version of narrative histories according to their political, economic, and cultural status.

Conclusion

From the analysis in this chapter, it is possible to say that there are many "facts" about the massacre and thus there are many interpretations concerning what caused it. From these various interpretations, people choose certain interpretations that best suit them, or the ones that are least harmful to their interests.

Expectedly, these narratives are not equally accepted in society. For obvious reasons, that of the local movement leaders became the dominant one, while the narratives of the attackers and the survivors occupy a subordinate position. Between the two, the Tiwas are creating their own social and political spaces through their demands for an autonomous district. At the same time, they are developing a counter-narrative about the violence, distinct from that of the Assamese. On the other hand, the voice of the Muslim immigrants is more subdued. Although they lament the casualty, they are not so vocal in criticizing the attackers. They neither have their own organizations nor the media to express their interests.

From the facts presented here, it can be said that a group's strategy has a significant influence on its narratives of the past, in this case, the memories of violence. The groups under consideration differ in the sense of whether they do, or choose not to, pursue their own identity. When they choose to establish themselves as distinct and separate from the dominant group, they need to narrate their own version of history, to define themselves as a subject in it, and to differentiate themselves from the dominant group. However, when it is impossible for them to differentiate themselves with the mainstream community, they are forced to assimilate with them and there is no option for them to develop their own history.

In this context, the Tiwas have already been in the process of establishing their own identity in order to attain an autonomous district. Although their demand for the autonomous district existed even before the movement, it was after the movement that the Tiwas became disappointed with the Assamese, the ATSU was formed, and they started a full-fledged movement to attain their autonomy. In this process, they needed to define themselves as different from the Assamese, and the experience of the Nellie massacre was interpreted in this context. They emphasize the betrayal by the Assamese people, and claim that the Assamese exploited the Tiwas to suit their own interest. Especially, they recall the bitter experience of being stereotyped as "wild tribes." In other words, through the experience of the Nellie incident and the Assam movement, the Tiwa people became aware of their exploited situation and decided to exercise their own agency—this time, through the movement for autonomy.

As for the Muslims, at the time of the research, they were still forced to assimilate into the dominant Assamese community. For them, it is not only unnecessary, but even harmful, to differentiate themselves from the indigenous Assamese society. Thus, they only referred to the direct cause of the Nellie massacre, and never used it like the Tiwas do to bolster their autonomous movement. There are fragments of narratives which mourn the tragedy they suffered, but they are scattered and without a place to be represented or to be spoken about by leaders.

This lack of a mobilized movement is not due to the Muslims of immigrant origin being less resourceful than the indigenous groups. In fact, the Muslims are larger in number and there is a new middle class emerging among them as in the case of the indigenous peoples. However, the Muslims are less enthusiastic in defining themselves as distinct from the Assamese and mobilizing a movement. The reasons are, first, being an immigrant group, the Muslims lack a territorial base in Assam. The second is their fear of the emergence of another movement or political move which could drive them out of Assam, particularly during the AGP regime. As argued in Chapter 5, the Muslims in India are easily targeted as an "enemy community" for they are alleged to have an extraterritorial association with Pakistan or Bangladesh. Particularly, in the case of the Muslims who have their origin in the Bengal region, because of their origin, they are easily suspected of being agents of Bangladesh. Thus, they are in a difficult position in relation to mobilizing a movement; therefore they choose (or are forced) to assimilate into the Assamese culture.

Until now, there has been no intensive examination of relationships between the narratives of history (especially those involving memories of violence) and the identity formation of ethnic minorities. From the analysis in this chapter, it can be said that the minorities have to choose whether or not to articulate their identities, especially when we make comparisons to established nations that have developed their official histories. This formation of collective identity has a strong influence on the development of counter-narratives against the official history of the dominant majority community. By examining the narratives on the Nellie massacre, we have seen that quite a different type of narrative emerged among the Tiwas and the Muslims of immigrant origin as compared to that of the Assamese middle class. The memories of the violence are diverse. The middle-class Assamese narratives are dominant in the society. The Tiwas' narrative contests the dominant narrative by establishing an alternative discourse. The narratives of the Muslims are fragmented, and never form a discourse effective enough to counter the dominant one. In the concluding chapter, based on my revisit to the area in 2007, I start with an analysis on their lack of political movement.

Notes

1. "Gherao" is an Indian term indicating an act of enclosing, shutting in, or surrounding.
2. During my one-month stay in Assam, the police visited me twice and told me not to make research visits without their accompanying me for "security reasons." In order to conduct research without their interference, I had to meet the deputy commissioner and report to the district's superintendent of police.
3. In the Nellie area, the interviews were conducted in Assamese through interpreters and in such places as Jagiroad or Morigaon, they were conducted in English. I did not make any corrections to grammatical mistakes, since I prefer to show the exact words that the interviewees used. The same goes for the interviews through interpreters, since I believe those are more suitable to express the situation at the time of the interview.
4. Group interview with villagers in village A, November 12, 2001.
5. Group interview with villagers in village B, November 23, 2001.
6. Group interview with villagers in village C, November 15, 2001.
7. Group interview with villagers in village D, November 24, 2001.
8. Group interview with villagers in village C, November 15, 2001.
9. Group interview with villagers in village D, November 24, 2001.
10. Interview with Mr X in Morigaon, November 21, 2001.
11. Interview with Mr Y in Morigaon, November 21, 2001.
12. Interview with Ms U in a village in Tetelia Tribal Block, November 15, 2001.
13. The Sixth Schedule of the Constitution of India states that a new autonomous district can be created by the Governor's public notification.
14. Interview with a former member of the Tiwa Autonomous Council in Nellie area, February 15, 2002; The Lalung Darbar, *Memorandum to Shri Rajiv Gandhi, Prime Minister of India, New Delhi* (November 10, 1987): 2–3.
15. *The Assam Gazette Extraordinary*, July 13, 1995; Autonomous Lalung District Demand Committee, *A Memorandum to Shri Hiteswar Saikia, Chief Minister of Assam*, May 10, 1993.

16. Interview with Tulsi Bordoloi, chairman of the ADSF, in Jagiroad, November 13, 2001.

17. Interviews with Udhab Senapati, the founder-president of the Tiwa Sahitya Sabha, in the Nellie area, February 15, 2002, and Tulsi Bordoloi, February 14, 2002.

18. Interview with Tulsi Bordoloi in Jagiroad, February 14, 2002.

7

Conclusion

Revisiting Nellie: August 2007

In August 2007, I had the chance to visit Nellie again to conduct interviews, mainly with the survivors of the attacks this time. It was six years after I had first conducted fieldwork there for my PhD research, and I observed important differences in people's reactions to my inquiries. The Muslim villagers were more vocal, and at the same time, some showed frustration about their situation. I quote from one such interview, with Sirajuddin, a resident of Nellie village.

"Everybody comes here with some purpose," Sirajuddin said irritated. I was puzzled at his reaction and looked at my research-partner–cum–interpreter.[1] He explained,

> You see, he is completely frustrated. The victims [of the Nellie massacre] were paid only 5,000 rupees in compensation. Indira Gandhi declared that if people were killed because they had gone to vote, they would be paid lakhs of compensation, but, obviously, the survivors did not get the money (400,000 rupees, added Sirajuddin). In the case of the Sikh victims killed in Delhi after the assassination of the prime minister, however, the families were compensated 700,000 rupees. So, what is the justification for raising the question of compensation now? Under the same government, we are compensated less, but other people are compensated more. Those who attacked us, they were given 35,000 rupees. He is feeling that there's no truth here.[2]

During the six years that had passed, there had been a series of changes in the situation surrounding the victims of the Nellie incident. In 2001, it was right after the Congress won the State Legislative Assembly election and came to back to power. People still had a fresh memory of the Asom

Gana Parishad (AGP) and were not very vocal to talk about the incident for fear of retaliation. However, in 2006, a political party claiming to represent the Muslims of immigrant origin emerged and secured 10 seats in the State Legislative Assembly election. The party requested the state government to make the Tewary Commission Report public, in order to request compensation for the Nellie massacre victims. In New Delhi, the Congress had returned to power the preceding year with Prime Minister Manmohan Singh from Punjab, and declared that it would provide compensation of 700,000 rupees for each of the victims of the 1984 anti-Sikh riots.

There were also new and updated reports on the incident. Hemendra Narayan, who had been a witness to the incident and had broken the story in the *Indian Express,* published—25 years later in 2008—a small booklet in which he recalled what had happened and collected documents showing different views on the incident, such as official reports and Tiwa Darbar's memorandum (Narayan 2008).

A few journalists had also visited the site, such as *Tehelka*'s Teresa Rehman, who reported on the situation. She also obtained the Tewary Commission Report and reported part of its findings on the Nellie incident, particularly regarding the negligence of duty on the part of police officers there. *India Today* also published a small article under "Greatest Stories Revisited" in its 30-year anniversary issue in December 2006 (Sen 2006). *The Hindu* published an article by Harsh Mander, who visited the site in November 2008 (Mander 2008).

Thus, the quiet villages in Nellie had seen some people coming and going, inquiring about the incident, but nothing had happened to make their lives happier or easier. Also, the fact that I was with an interpreter from the same community might have given them some confidence and sense of security. Sirajuddin's statement of irritation emerged under these circumstances.

When we left Sirajuddin's house, and proceeded to two affected villages— Muladhari and Alichinga—we were able to understand his sentiments in part. After a six-year period, it appeared that not much had changed in the villages, and that there were no improvements in the people's lives. Actually, this was my first visit to the area during the monsoon season. After taking a turn off the national highway and proceeding on the village road, the driver of our hired car began to complain about the road's condition. There had been a flood several days earlier, and there were makeshift huts on the narrow road on the embankment. After traveling a few kilometers, the driver refused to go further. We were about to start walking when a person passing by offered to take us on his motorbike.

When we reached the village, some parts of it seemed to be submerged in the river. In Assam's rural areas, flood-prone areas near the river are often underwater for several days, and sometimes weeks, during the rainy season. The Muslim villages are located just south of the Kopili River, and the pond, locally known as *beel* (swamp), expands during the rainy season. Though the villages were just a few kilometers away from the main road, they were just as inaccessible as remote *char* and forest areas. It is no wonder that this flood-prone area was left vacant till the 1930s, when immigrants began to move away from the riverbank of the Brahmaputra and down to the southern part of the district in search of land.

Apart from several health centers and lower primary schools, there were no new facilities in the villages. Partly because of the lack of access to higher education, even six years ago, it was very difficult to find a research assistant from the community who could communicate in English. Thus, during my first research trip in 2001–2002, I had to rely on Tiwa or Assamese Hindu interpreters, and partly because of this, the survivors of the riot were not willing to share their experiences.

When we reached the Nellie area, we first went to Muladhari and started with an interview with a schoolteacher in the village. It was a hot and humid day, and the teacher offered us the back area of the house on the riverbank, where the bamboo trees blocked the sunshine. It was a quiet afternoon where we could talk with several villagers sitting on the banks of the river, which had been blocked during the attack on that fateful day. Under the bamboo trees, we began the interviews.

The difference in the attitude of the people in Muladhari village compared to my first field visit was apparent. Villagers were more vocal and outspoken about the loss of life in their own families. For example, a schoolteacher in the village recounted as follows:

> In my family, including all my relatives, more than 70 people died. My mother-in-law and grandmother, auntie, nephews and nieces.... On that day, the attack started at about eight in the morning. They started to light the houses on fire and came towards us from different directions. After burning down the houses, they started to kill the people. We assembled in the field and started to run towards the Kiling River. About 10 CRPF personnel were stationed in the [western] direction. While we were running, many were killed from behind. Those able to reach the CRPF camp were able to survive.[3]

While we were talking, Saidul from Alichinga village started to talk.

> My brothers and grandfather were also killed on that day. My mother was
> pierced with something like an arrow 26 times, but was treated and cured.
> Altogether, 17 people from my family lost their lives.[4]

Another person listening to our interview added his experience.

> Three of my younger brothers were killed. Another brother got shot and the
> bullet went into his forehead. He had an operation at a hospital in Nagaon
> and they were able to save his life.[5]

A blind man came. He had been shot with a handmade gun, and nine bullets
had gone into his left shoulder. He later lost his eyesight. He lost his son
and father in the incident.

These statements could go on and on. There were approximately
6,000–7,000 Muslim villagers in the area, and at least 2,000 lost their lives.
No family in this area was spared from the loss of life. Any person in the
village you come across can tell a similar story of the loss of human life in
his/her family. The most astonishing thing about the situation in Nellie is
that despite this huge loss of life, most people went back to their villages
and continued to live with the neighbors who had lent a hand in the attack.
Usually, in the case of communal riots concerning land issues, the survivors
of an attack cannot return to their houses or villages for fear of another attack.
The situation in Nellie is partly due to the efforts of the Congress government,
which provided security by setting up an army patrol right after the incident.

The survivors in the Nellie area were vocal not only on the loss of their
family members and properties, but also about who were responsible for
the attack. Some mentioned that the All Assam Students' Union (AASU)
and the All Assam Gana Sangram Parishad (AAGSP) were responsible.
Such testimonies were not available during my first research trip. On my
first visit, the villagers stressed that as Assamese, they too had supported
the movement, but they had been mistaken for foreigners and had become
the target of attack. Others too frankly stated that the officer-in-charge of
Jagiroad Police Station had tried to mislead the Central Reserve Police Force
(CRPF) personnel from proceeding to the villages. A Muslim woman in Nellie
village, however, shouted out to show them the right way, and because of
this, the troop was able to reach the site of the attack. They also noted that

many people used guns in the attack, which must have been obtained from the local Assam police battalions.

People also lamented that although the late Indira Gandhi and the government had made promises for relief to and the development of the village, this had not been sufficient. For example,

> Indira Gandhi assured us of rebuilding the houses, but nothing happened afterwards. There were small improvements in roads, communications and electricity, but apart from that, nothing has changed since 1983.
>
> The families of those who were killed received only 5,000 rupees. However, those on the attacking side received 35,000 rupees. We went to the polls since the Congress assured us safety, but nothing happened.
>
> There are no educated people from this village. We do not know where to go even if we want to do something. We just received 5,000 rupees and they received 35,000 rupees. There is no use asking for justice.[6]

Further, in an interview in another village, people frequently mentioned Indira Gandhi's name when talking about the killings.

> Indira Gandhi told us to vote. When she came here [after the massacre], she told us, "What happened has already happened, but you should not leave this place. I shall offer every possible help, for fixing and maintaining your houses. Whatever it is, I am here with you and I shall help you. Don't worry."
>
> She also said that she would make it an ideal village. Houses and roads would be constructed. Hospitals would be constructed. Schools would be constructed, and a police station would be constructed. But we only got 2,000 rupees and three bundles of tin for roofs.
>
> When we escaped, we only had the sarees we wore. All the goats and cows are gone. There was no food, nothing. The government only offered 500 rupees to buy some cattle and bullocks.[7]

Such sentiments of the villagers are articulated in Sirajuddin's account, which I introduced in the first part of this chapter. Sirajuddin has played an important role in representing the voice of the local people since the violence took place. He formed an organization for relief and rehabilitation for the Nellie massacre and became its president, and he collected data on the number of the deceased and the injured from the area. He was an interviewee for both the official inquiry committee (Tewary Commission) and a non-official inquiry committee (Mehta Commission). He has also been a signatory to the memorandum submitted to the Government of India (GOI) in 2007, which asked for compensation and development in the village.

The Politics of Compensation and the Alienation of the Muslims in Assam's Politics

This was not the first time that a memorandum asking for relief, rehabilitation and development for the survivors of the killing was submitted to the government. The first was submitted in 1983 right after the killing, and another in 1991. The 1983 memorandum asked for the construction of a state-maintained public road, embankment, provisions of rations and cloth, and the establishment of a hospital and schools, and was submitted by seven individual signatories. All memoranda were submitted when there had been a change in government and the Congress had come to power. In 1983 it was, of course, right after the incident and right after the Congress came to power in the state. In 1991 it was when the Congress regained power in the state after five years of AGP rule. During the AGP's rule, all criminal cases filed relating to the incidents had been dropped.

In 1991, the villagers formed the "Action Committee for Relief and Rehabilitation of Riot Victims Minority Peoples 1983" and requested the government to declare the victims as *swahid* (martyrs). The group also asked for proper compensation by citing the example of compensation paid to the Bodo people, and asked for eight *bigha*s (one-third of an acre) of land for each affected family. They also requested the government to provide roads, electricity, water, an irrigation system, a primary health center, madrassa and mosques, and other infrastructure. Although the 1991 memorandum put more emphasis on compensation and the declaration of victims as swahid, many of their requests were the same as those made in the 1983 memorandum.

In the memorandum submitted in 1991, the survivors mentioned the government's payment of 100,000 rupees to each of the victims in the Bodo areas affected.

It may be mentioned that the ex-gratia payment by the former AGP government in 1985 to the deceased of the affected Bodo areas was Rs 5,000 each. But the present government has again provided the Bodo people with Rs 1 lakh each as ex gratia payment, leaving aside the families of victims of the Nellie area, who are mainly a minority community. We, the people of the Nellie area, are getting no justice as requested from the Chief Minister by granting Rs 1 lakh each to the families of the victims.[8]

The difference in the amount of compensation is still an issue in Assam politics. In 2007, when 48 Hindi-speaking migrant workers (especially those from Bihar State) in Assam were attacked in the upper Assam districts, political leaders rushed to upper Assam and declared that they would give compensation to each victim's next of kin. The Samajwadi party provided 100,000 rupees immediately after the incident, while the Assam government announced an amount of 300,000 rupees, Prime Minister Manmohan Singh an additional ex gratia of 200,000 rupees, and the Bihar government 100,000 rupees. As a result, the families of each victim were entitled to receive a total amount of 700,000 rupees—more than double the compensation of 300,000 rupees paid to the families of victims of killings in the Karbi–Dimasa clash in Karbi Anglong and North Cachar Hills in the state. Having pointed out that the political parties were trying to garner political mileage out of the situation, journalist Sushanta Talukdar commented, "Such politics of compensation, however, will only result in legitimizing the regional divide, which ULFA [the United Liberation Front of Asom] sought to bring in by targeting migrants" (Talukdar 2007).

Such politics of compensation is seen in pan-Indian politics, as well. In 2005–2006, the GOI declared that it would pay ex gratia of 700,000 rupees to the victims of the anti-Sikh riots in 1984. It should be noted that this decision was made after Manmohan Singh, the first Sikh to become prime minister of India, came to the post in 2004. The GOI also declared that it would give compensation to the victims of the Gujarat riots in 2002, the recipients mainly the Muslims, the traditional vote bank of the Congress party. It can be noted that political parties use the issue of compensation in order to garner political support.

The content of the memorandum submitted in 2007 by 16 residents of the attacked villages in the Nellie area was more or less similar to previous ones, asking for the provision of basic facilities such as drinking water, roads, mosques and madrassas, primary schools, houses, electricity, a hospital and a bridge. However, it referred to the decision of the central government in 2006 to provide 700,000 rupees in compensation in regard to the 1984 massacres of the Sikhs in Delhi following the assassination of Indira Gandhi.

In this regard, the memorandum pointed out the disparity in compensation and asked for a uniform policy.

Reading the statement, one might feel it odd that the survivors of the massacre asked for compensation, instead of requesting proper judicial procedure and punishment for the attackers. In a way, the survivors also use the same logic and language as the government and political parties. In order to understand this, we need to take into consideration the fact that most of the attackers in incidents of collective violence in India are left unidentified and unpunished. This is deeply related to the issue of impunity in contemporary India. Most attackers, or people in power and in charge of security at the time, are rarely punished for large-scale violence. In the case of the Nellie incident too, no one was punished for the large-scale attack during the State Legislative Assembly election in 1983. Six hundred cases were filed in relation to the incident, but when the student leaders came to power, all were dropped. Both the movement leaders who had organized the boycott and the Congress who had forced the election did not take any responsibility for the disturbance and loss of life.

The survivors in the affected villages are, on the one hand, very practical in what they demand in their memoranda. From their point of view, they voted in the election as requested by Indira Gandhi; hence, they feel that proper compensation should be paid by the Congress government, and thus, whenever the Congress comes to power in the state, as well as in the central government, they repeat their demand for compensation. When the survivors in the Nellie area request compensation, we have to understand that this demand is made within this political context, and also that their political action is very limited.

This does not mean that the survivors are not interested in any judicial persecution or justice. Sirajuddin, who continues to organize the people and submit memoranda for compensation, strongly stated,

> From my own family and relatives, 47 lost their lives. I lost my parents and four daughters. There should be some kind of justice when such grave crime is committed. However, here in Assam, nothing happened after the massacre. If there's no justice provided, then we have to bring justice about.[9]

There are also reports that other survivors also hope for a proper hearing in a court of law (Rehman 2006). However, it is difficult to articulate such desire for justice in ways different from asking for compensation, since they are still a minority in the area and some of the attackers live side by side with them. Also, the Muslims of immigrant origin are still marginalized and often stigmatized as "outsiders" in Assamese society.

The foreigner issue is still one of the most important on the political agenda in Assam. When the AGP came to power in the state in 1985 and 1996, they could not provide a political solution for it. The Muslims already comprised more than 25 percent of the population, and the AGP was aware that without their support, the party would not be able to maintain its base in Assam. Thus, in contrast to Muslim expectations, no large-scale deportation took place during the AGP regime. However, the movement against "illegal immigrants" or "Bangladeshi" infiltration remained, and both the AGP and the AASU garnered support by propagating fear among the Assamese Hindus.

The antiforeigner movement alienated the Muslims in the politics in Assam, reinforcing the situation of the Muslims needing to rely on the Congress. For example, at the time of the elections, many Muslims of immigrant origin were marked as "D" (doubtful) voters and harassed to not vote. Though most have lived in Assam for three generations, they are still stigmatized as "foreigners" and "outsiders." The Congress has benefited from this situation, where the Muslims are alienated and have their security threatened, by playing the role of "protectors of the minority" to gain the vote bank. However, politicians use the Muslims only at election time, and have done hardly anything to uplift their status in Assam.

In 2006, with the emergence of the Assam United Democratic Front (AUDF) only three months before the State Legislative Assembly election, there was a slight change in politics surrounding the Muslims. Although claiming to be secular, and to aim to represent all minorities in the state, with Badruddin Ajmal, a Muslim of immigrant origin, as its president, the AUDF received the strong support of the Muslims, and the party secured 10 seats in the Assembly election. The working president of the party, Hafiz Rashid Ahmed Choudhury, demanded the publication of the Tewary Commission Report, a judicial inquiry commission report that has remained unpublished for two decades. This may have encouraged the survivors of the Nellie incident and provided them with an impetus for submitting a memorandum in 2007. However, thus far, the Tewary Commission Report is not yet public. Whether the AUDF can be a party that represents the interests of the Muslims is still unclear, and so far, no drastic change has taken place regarding the situation in Nellie.

Two Discourses of Assamese Nationalism and a Challenge by Indigenous Movements since 1985

After the Assam Accord was signed and the AASU leaders formed a political party (the AGP), which came into power in 1985, there emerged other types of nationalist movements in Assam. Right after the Assam Accord, the ULFA became very active and influential in its armed struggle. The ULFA's main claim was that Assam was not part of India and should seek independence. In their claims, the ULFA included the Muslims of immigrant origin as part of the Assamese nation. Because of their activities, hostility towards the Muslims and division among the communities were, to some extent, weakened (Saikia 2004: 171–72).

The reason for the ULFA's claim for independence can be understood considering the GOI's attitude towards the Assam movement: even for legitimate claims and peaceful satyagrahas, the GOI used the police and security forces to disperse and suppress the movement, which the ULFA also participated actively in. As argued earlier, the immigration problem is not unique to Assam; it has been a common phenomenon in decolonized countries where the demography changed substantially during the colonial period. However, the difference in Assam's case was that immigration continued even after independence, and the Assamese people did not have the authority to regulate the population flow. Thus, if we take a look at the antiforeigner movement, it is apparent that the legitimate claims of the student leaders were not accepted by the GOI.

With the birth of the AGP as a political party, the antiforeigner movement in Assam became more or less institutionalized in Assamese politics. The AGP still keeps the foreigner issue as one of the party's main agenda items, but it could not propose a way to detect and deport foreigners without harassing the descendants of the Muslims from East Bengal, nor could it seek political settlement. In a way, the antiforeigner and anti-Bangladeshi slogans became a mere political tool for the AGP to differentiate itself from the ruling Congress party. The same can be said of the AASU, which keeps raising the issue without practical political orientation, or challenging the present order and the state. It criticizes the AGP but never challenges their lack of will for effective solution to the problem. The organization has lost some kind of support from the people, which it had enjoyed during the antiforeigner movement.

Under these circumstances, the security of the Muslims in the state has been threatened for a long time. Although there have not been large-scale killings such as the Nellie incident, whenever the elections come around, the antiforeigner and anti-Bangladeshi slogans emerge. Major political parties in Assam, including the Congress, do not have the will to solve the problem, and only take advantage of the issue; the AGP and the Bharatiya Janata Party (BJP) use it to emphasize the threat to the Assamese middle class and, hence, attract their vote, and the Congress, on the other hand, uses the opportunity to play the role of protector of the Muslims without really securing their safety, and without any concrete policy or will to solve the issue.

With the emergence of the ULFA movement, the fear of being overwhelmed by immigrants, which the AASU and the AGP had used to increase nationalistic support, ceased to be the only nationalist discourse in Assamese society. Since the late 1980s, another discourse on Assamese nationality has emerged—one emphasizing the colonization of Assam by India (Baruah 1999). The ULFA's Assamese nationalism was a fusion of three different nationalisms: (1) military tradition, (2) revivalism, typified by the likes of the Ahom revivalists, and (3) leftist traditions. Due to the GOI's Operation Rhino and Operation Bajrang, the ULFA's influence has decreased considerably, but the idea still has some support in Assam. During this period (late 1980s to 1990s/2000s), the anti-immigration issue has remained important in Assamese society, particularly when it comes to electoral politics.

From the 1990s, the BJP has been successful in creating some organizational basis in Assamese politics. The party secured four seats in the 1996 State Legislative Assembly election, eight seats in 2001, and ten seats in 2006. It sealed seat-sharing agreements with the AGP in the 2001 State Legislative Assembly election and the 2009 Lok Sabha election. The AGP's anti-immigration propaganda echoed some of the BJP's anti-Muslim propaganda. For example, the BJP brought the anti-Bangladeshi rhetoric to an all-India level by stating that a huge number of migrant Bangladeshis were in the country (Saikia 2004: 66). As a result of the institutionalization of the immigration issue in elections, an outburst of violence against the Muslims, seen at the time of the State Legislative Assembly election in 1983, was not seen after the Assam Accord.

The violence before and after the election period in Assam in 1983 was marked by an outbreak of distrust and dissatisfaction towards the Congress government by the rural masses. This was not only a result of propaganda by the AASU; the threat was commonly felt among the rural villagers in Assam.

In particular, the Muslim expansion and loss of land was felt very acutely by indigenous peoples in the state. These circumstances led to support of the AASU not only by the caste-Hindu Assamese, but also by the indigenous peoples and other communities in the lower Hindu strata.

However, after the Assam Accord, the indigenous peoples, especially those in the plains, started their own movement. They were disappointed at the fact that the movement leaders had merely utilized the issue of land alienation for mobilization, and that they did not achieve much fruitful results in the end. It is notable that in the Assam Accord, it was stated that there would be a constitutional measure to strengthen Assamese identity, but there was no mention of the issue of indigenous/tribal identity. Moreover, under the clause relating to the protection of government land, the Accord put indigenous peoples at the risk of being evicted from their forest homes.

The movement for autonomy carried out by the indigenous tribal groups had made an appearance even before the antiforeigner movement. The change that came after the movement was not only a reinforcement of the demand for autonomy in social and economic development, but a conscious attempt by the group to differentiate itself from people of Assamese nationality. Today, indigenous peoples, who comprise only 10 percent of the total population of Assam, are major challengers of the Assamese nationality led by the caste-Hindu middle-class Assamese.

The most influential movement led by the Bodos seeks a separate state, which was partly fulfilled by creation of Bodo Territorial Council after the signing of the second Bodo Accord in 2003. Other indigenous groups also started their own movements for autonomy. Apart from the Hill indigenous groups, who began their movement much earlier, the Tiwas, Mishings, Rabhas, Sonowals, and many other groups in the plain areas started movements in the late 1980s and became very active in the 1990s. Some narratives of the Tiwa villagers in Chapter 6 illustrate that the indigenous peoples support their own nationalism, rather than a greater Assamese nationalism, and this is partly because of their dissatisfaction with and disbelief of the middle-class and caste-Hindu Assamese leadership.

Although their claims for territorial autonomy can be justified considering the historical process of their loss of land and autonomy, because of the long history of immigration and interdistrict movement, the population in Assam is largely mixed and it is difficult to demarcate the area where indigenous groups are dominant in the plains of the state. Thus, soon after the indigenous groups began to negotiate for an autonomous district, violent clashes started to take place in many areas where movements for autonomy or independence were active. For instance, there was an attack against the Muslims and the Adivasis (the Santhals, the Mundas, and the Oraons, who are also indigenous peoples in Jharkhand/Chotanagpur area but migrated to Assam during the colonial period. Many came as workers in tea plantations.) by Bodo armed groups in the mid-1990s, right after the first Bodo Accord in 1993. In 1994, the Muslims in Barpeta District were targeted and 68 people were killed, displacing 70,000 more (Chaudhuri 1994: 28). In 1996, violence spurred against the Adivasis, displacing 42,214 families, or 202,684 people. Again, in 1998, in a clash between the Bodos and the Adivasis, 48 people were killed in Kokrajhar District and 70,000 people took shelter in 28 relief camps in total (Chaudhuri 1998).

From September to October 2005, a Karbi–Dimasa clash took place in Karbi Anglong District in the middle section of Assam. In one month, the violence claimed at least 87 lives and rendered nearly 50,000 people homeless. The rivalry between the United People's Democratic Solidarity, an organization seeking the promotion of Karbi nationalism in Karbi Anglong District, and Dima Halim Daogah of neighboring North Cachar Hills, seeking to achieve a separate state for the Dimasa people, is said to have caused the clashes. Both organizations entered into a ceasefire agreement with the GOI in 2002–2003 (Talukdar 2005).

In October 2008, there was a series of attacks against the Muslims in the north bank of the Brahmaputra river, after the ceasefire between the central government and the National Democratic Front of Bodoland, and negotiation for peace began in 2005. The attacks killed 55 people, the majority of them Muslims of immigrant origin; but they also killed some indigenous peoples, including the Bodos. Through these killings, 54 villages were affected and 2,505 houses burnt down, and more than 200,000 people rushed to the relief camps (Talukdar 2008).

Unlike the election violence in 1983, which was unexpected for almost everybody, the pattern of violence today is more or less fixed, and has became routinized. Regarding the ethnic killings in the 1990s and 2000s, it is clear that there is the involvement of armed groups in most cases but in some cases, the local residents also lent a hand. At the same time, in such attacks, displacement of the "Other" community itself becomes part of the objective of the killings. Death tolls are smaller, but the number of Internally Displaced Persons (IDPs) is large (50,000 to hundreds of thousands of villagers are affected) and their displacement continues longer. In terms of the attacks during the Bodoland movement, many IDPs have spent almost two decades and still do not have any scope to go back or get resettled in a proper place with cultivable land. Thus, although large-scale killings did not take place after the Nellie massacre, different types of violence against the minorities in Assam continue even today.

Conclusion

The people in Assam and many other parts of South Asia are subject to "riots," which seem like unorganized and spontaneous violence. The analyses in this book and many other studies on collective violence show that such style of violence can take place anywhere if certain political conditions are met. In other words, in contemporary South Asia, anyone can become a victim of collective violence. More importantly, it is possible for anyone to become an attacker in collective violence.

Most of the collective violence in India is triggered and caused by political parties, large-scale organizations promoting ethnic or religious nationalist movements, and in some cases, armed organizations. There are cases of influential politicians instigating violence and using *goonda*s, criminals, or the urban poor to carry out their plans. Some local politicians and leaders seize the opportunity and utilize such occasions of violence. However, as analyzed in the case of the Nellie incident and many other incidents of large-scale collective violence, ordinary people are also involved. To regard only riot participants as fanatics, religious fundamentalists and criminal elements, would overlook some of the aspects of collective violence.

My analysis of the Nellie incident has revealed that the conditions for people to make the decision to participate in riots include: (1) The distinction between the enemy and "us" is demarcated along ethnic lines. (2) People feel acute threats to their security due to small-scale disturbances preceding the riots. (3) People know that for certain reasons, the law-enforcement agencies will not work against them. In the narratives of the riot participants in the Nellie incident, the second point was the most emphasized and considered important in decision making.

There were many factors that contributed to the violence, namely, the issue of land alienation, the election, and the antiforeigner movement. However, when ordinary people decide to participate in the violence, despite it being against their morals or in the face of community opposition, they need to have specific reasons. Regarding the Nellie incident, some people tried to take the opportunity to drive the Muslims out in order to take their land or gain political advantage. At the same time, the acute threat they felt to their security was the most important factor overriding the risk of being legally sanctioned, and to persuade people who opposed the attacks to participate.

In other words, in South Asia, people participate in riots because they are the only way for them to protect themselves or their property, and no one else, including state law-enforcement agencies, will protect them. And the situation that the people are placed in is often created by politicians, religious or ethnic leaders, or armed organizations. A focus on the agency of the rioters has revealed that they are often members of a more vulnerable segment of society, and that their situation is often not too different from that of the people they attack. In fact, if conditions were just a little different, the rioters would have been positioned on the opposite side, as victims instead of perpetrators of the attack.

Another important finding in the study of the agency of rioters is that in the Nellie incident, the distrust and the anger towards the Congress government was widely shared by the local people in the area. The issue of land alienation caused by immigration had been a long-standing problem since the colonial period. However, the Congress government, which at the time had ruled Assam for more than three decades, did not take any effective measures to address it. Rather, the government oppressed the antiforeigner movement. Whether the people supported the movement or not, the problems caused by large-scale immigration were widely felt among the Assamese people, and the government's oppression of the movement leaders invited distrust from the local people, including the indigenous tribal groups. Such distrust of the authorities was also an important factor for people in their decision on whether or not to participate in the riots.

The Nellie incident was definitely an occasion when peasants, including the indigenous peoples and other marginalized groups such as the Kochs and the Hiras, showed their will to challenge the situation, deciding to participate in the riot. This did challenge the central government and the election forced by the state. However, looking at the situation after the election and after the Assam Accord in 1985, their rebellion did not result in meaningful change, nor did their initiative continue for a long period of time. It was a sporadic attack that occurred during an extreme situation, and it did not bring about a revolution or cause real change in the structure of society. Indigenous peoples and other marginalized communities, however, took some initiatives to find a space and raise their voices in the autonomy movements that became prominent from the late 1980s and continue today.

However, the movement seeking autonomy does not seem to have achieved the goals it aimed for. Both the government, as well as the former movement leaders who entered politics, have failed to provide effective measures for the issue of land alienation and immigration, which were the primary concerns of the people who supported the movement. Furthermore, the issue triggered a number of ethnic genocides in many parts of Assam, as argued here.

On the other hand, the Muslims, who were not very vocal at the time my research was conducted in 2001 and 2002, renewed their demand for compensation to the Congress-led GOI after the change of regime. From the narratives of the survivors, it is apparent that they feel that there should be justice regarding the Nellie incident. In the Nellie area, there is no visible confrontation between the communities, but for both the attackers and the survivors, the issues of land alienation and immigration, and remedies for the survivors, remain unresolved.

In this area, both the survivors and the attackers live side by side with one another—just across the Kopili River, or a national highway, or sometimes in the same village. This is certainly a painful situation for the survivors, but also for the attackers, who have to face the outcome of their attack and negotiate with their memories that they are the attackers.

When the government does not come up with any effective solution to the issue, what can be done? Compensation, which the survivors of the Nellie incident ask for, might not bring about a meaningful solution to the problem. Instead, what is necessary today is to talk and negotiate with neighboring groups and try to seek a peaceful resolution with them. If the leaders of the autonomous movements seek not only political status and benefits, but also real solutions to the issues that the indigenous groups face on the ground, especially that of the right to live without fear, then, constructive and peaceful negotiation with other groups in the territory is required. In the case of past killings such as the Nellie incident, reconciliation among the communities concerned is likely to bring positive change in the situation. Thus, although there is no denying the fact that official judicial persecution or compensation are important steps towards the resolution of the problem, truth-telling commissions and reconciliation among communities as conducted in countries that experienced large-scale killings (such as South Africa, Guatemala, and Rwanda) might contribute more successfully towards a solution.

As has been argued in this book, the Nellie massacre was partly an outcome of an initiative by grassroots communities to riot. This can be solved only through people's initiatives. I just hope that in the future, the initiatives of peasants in rural areas will lead to constructive and peaceful negotiations with their neighbors.

Notes

1. I thank Rejauld Karim, my research partner and interpreter, for accompanying me to Nellie and conducting research together. His insights and advice were helpful in understanding the political situation surrounding the Muslims of immigrant origin in Assam.
2. Interview with Sirajuddin, 61 years old, in Nellie village, August 19, 2007.
3. Interview with Omar Ali, 34 years old, Muladhari village, August 17, 2007.
4. Interview with Saidul (age unknown), Alichinga village, August 17, 2007
5. Interview with a villager (name and age unknown), Muladhari village, August 17, 2007.
6. Group interview with villagers in Muladhari village, August 17, 2007.
7. Group interview with villagers in Alichinga village, August 19, 2007.
8. *A Memorandum submitted to the Prime Minister of India by Action Committee for Relief and Rehabilitation of Riot Victims Minority Peoples 1983*, submitted on September 1, 1991.
9. Interview with Sirajuddin, 61 years old, in Nellie village, August 19, 2007.

Bibliography

1. Primary Sources

A. Reports and Census of the Government

Census of India (1931) Assam.

Census of India (1951) Assam, Manipur and Tripura.

Census of India (1961) Assam.

Census of India (1971) Assam.

Census of India (1991) Series 4, Assam.

Census of India (2001) Provisional Population Totals: Figures at a Glance for Assam.

Assam District Gazetteers—Volume VI: Nowgong (1905).

Village Note: Mauza Laharighat (1931).

Report of the Line System Committee (1938), Shillong: Assam Government Press.

The Forest Resources of Assam (1940), Shillong: Assam Government Press.

Report of the Special Officer Appointed for the Examination of the Professional Grazing Reserves in the Assam Valley (1944), Shillong: Assam Government Press.

Delegation of Members of Parliament to Assam, Report (1960), New Delhi: Lok Sabha Secretariat.

The Assam Official Language Act, 1960 (Published in the *Assam Gazette*, Extraordinary, dated December 19, 1960).

A Study on The Assam Official Language Bill, 1960 (as passed by the Assam Legislative Assembly on October 24, 1960).

Report of the Commission of Inquiry into the Goreshwar Disturbances (1961), Shillong: Assam Government Press.

Statement of Shri Lal Bahadur Shastri, Union Home Minister, Shillong, June 6, 1961.

Press in India (1980–1986), New Delhi: Office of the Registrar of Newspapers for India.

Assam Gazette, Extraordinary, July 14, 1983.

DAVP (Directorate of Advertising and Visual Publicity). 1983. *Assam Events in Perspective.*

Tewary Commission Report (*Report of the Commission of Enquiry on Assam Disturbance, 1983*) (1984), Dispur: Assam Government Press.

The Assam Accord (Memorandum of Settlement) (1985).

B. Pamphlets

All Assam Students' Union (AASU). 1980a. *Voice of AASU: Mass Upheaval in Assam.* Guwahati: AASU.

———. 1980b. *Memorandum to the Prime Minister of India on Problem of Foreign Nationals in Assam.* Guwahati: AASU.

———. 1983a. *The Foreigners Problem: Why a Solution is Still Elusive?* Guwahati: AASU.

———. 1983b. *Today's Assam: A Graveyard of Democracy.* Guwahati: AASU.

———. 1983c. *A Farce-Election.* Guwahati: AASU.

———. (n.d.). *AASU's Viewpoints and Central Government's Attitude Regarding the Problem of Foreign Nationals.* Guwahati: AASU.

AASU and All Assam Gana Sangram Parishad (AAGSP). 1980. *Save Assam Today to Save India Tomorrow.* Guwahati: AASU.

Asam Sahitya Sabha. 1980. *Eclipse in the East: An Analysis of the Present Agitation in Assam.*

Assam College Teachers' Association. 1980. *Memorandum to the President of India.* Guwahati.

Assam Freedom Fighters' Association. 1980. *Assam's Struggle for Survival.* Guwahati.

———. 1985. *Report of the Non-Official Judicial Inquiry Commission on Holocaust of Assam Before, During, and After Election, 1983* (Mehta Commission Report). Guwahati.

Asom Jagriti. 1980. *Indian Citizens vs Foreign Nationals.* Guwahati.

Bengalee Community of the District of Assam, Nowgong. 1960. *Recent Tragedy in Assam: Memorandum to All Members of the Parliament.*

Borgohain, Homen. 2001. "Address of the President," *Sixty-sixth Session of Asam Sahitya Sabha,* February 9.

Cachar Language Victims Relief and Security Committee, Silchar (Assam). 1960. *Memorandum Submitted to the Parliamentary Delegation on 16-8-'60.*

Choudhury, J. K. 1948. *A Plan for Purbachal.*

Communist Party of India (Marxist). 1980. *Real Face of the Assam Agitation.*

CRPC. 1985. *The Assam Agreement and its Likely Fallout.* Guwahati.

Gauhati University Teachers' Association. 1980. *Invasion in Disguise: The Problem of Foreign Infiltration into Assam.*

Indian Citizens' Right Preservation Committee. 1980. *Assam Triangle: Facts and Myths.*

Junior Doctors' Association and Gauhati Medical College Students' Union. 1980a. *Will These Lives Go in Vain?* Guwahati: AASU.

———. 1980b. *Will You Let Us Live too?* Guwahati: AASU.

Neog, Maheswar (ed.). 1961. *Assam's Language Question: A Symposium.* Asam Sahitya Sabha.

———. 1974. "Presidential Address," *Forty-first Annual Conference of Asam Sahitya Sabha,* Mangaldai, February 9.

Purbanchaliya Lok Parishad. 1978. *PLP's Document No-3.*

C. Newspapers

Amrita Bazar Patrika, Kolkata
Ananda Bazar Patrika, Kolkata
Asom Bani, Guwahati
Dainik Assam, Guwahati
Hindustan Times, Delhi
Indian Express, Delhi
Telegraph, Kolkata
The Assam Tribune, Guwahati
The Statesman, Kolkata
Times of India, Mumbai

2. Secondary Sources

A. Books and Articles

Abbi, B. L. (ed.). 1984. *Northeast Region: Problems and Prospects of Development.* Chandigarh: Centre for Research in Rural and Industrial Development.

Ahmed, Abu Said & Adil-ul Yasin. 1997. "Problems of Identity, Assimilation and Nation-Building: A Case Study of the Muslims of Assam," in Girin Phukan & N. L. Dutta (eds), *Politics of Identity and Nation-Building in North-East India.* Dibrugarh: Dibrugarh University.

Amin, Shahid. 1995. *Event, Metaphor, Memory: Chauri Chaura 1922–1992.* Berkeley, CA: University of California Press.

Anderson, Benedict. 1983. *Imagined Communities: Reflections on the Origin and Spread of Nationalism.* London: Verso.

Annamalai, E. 2001. *Managing Multilingualism in India: Political and Linguistic Manifestations.* New Delhi: SAGE.

Ashcroft, Bill, Gareth Griffins & Helen Tiffin (eds). 1995. *The Post-Colonial Studies Reader.* London: Routledge.

Bakshi, S. R., S. R. Sharma, & S. Gajrani. 1998. *Prafulla Kumar Mahanta: Chief Minister of Assam.* New Delhi: APH Publishing.

Balakrishnan, Gopal (ed.). 1996. *Mapping the Nation.* London: Verso.

Barman, Santo. 1994. *Zamindari System in Assam during British Rule (A Case Study of Goalpara District).* Guwahati: Spectrum.

Barooah, D. P. 1984a. "India's North-Eastern Region and Problems of National Integration," in S. A. H. Haqqi (ed.), *Democracy, Pluralism and Nation-Building*, pp. 221–41. Delhi: NBO Publishers.

Barooah, D. P. 1984b. "Silent Civilian Invasion: India's Danger in the Northeast", in B. L. Abbi (ed.), *Northeast Region: Problems and Prospects of Development*, pp. 287–300. Chandigarh: Centre for Research in Rural and Industrial Development.

Barth, Frederik (ed.). 1969. *Ethnic Groups and Boundaries: The Social Organization of Culture of Differences*. Boston: Little, Brown and Company.

Barua, Hem. 1962. *The Red River and the Blue Hill* (revised and enlarged). Guwahati: Lawyer's Book Stall.

Barua, Indrani. 1990. *Pressure Groups in Assam*. New Delhi: Omsons.

Baruah, Sanjib Kumar. 1980. "Games Academics Play," *Mainstream*, 18 (30): 33–34.

————. 1999. *India Against Itself: Assam and Politics of Nationality*. Philadelphia: University of Pennsylvania Press.

Baruah, Sanjib. 2005. *Durable Disorder: Understanding the Politics of Northeast India*. New Delhi: Oxford University Press.

Basu, Sajal. 1992. *Regional Movements: Politics of Language, Ethnicity–Identity*. Shimla: Indian Institute of Advanced Study.

————. 2000. *Communalism, Ethnicity and State Politics*. Jaipur: Rawat.

Becker, C. 1989/1923. *Early History of the Catholic Missions in Northeast India* (transl. and ed. by F. Leicht SDS and S. Karotemprel SDB). Shillong: Firma KLM.

Beiner, Ronald. 1999. *Theorizing Nationalism*. Albany, NY: State University of New York Press.

Bertaux, Daniel. 1997. *Les Recits de Vie: Perspective Ethnosociologique*. Paris: VUEF.

Bordoloi, B. N. (ed.). 1986. *Alienation of Tribal Land and Indebtedness*. Guwahati: Tribal Research Institute, Assam.

————. 1999. *Report on the Survey of Alienation of Tribal Land in Assam*. Guwahati: Assam Institute of Research for Tribals and Scheduled Castes.

Borgohain, Homen. 2001. *Address of the President, Sixty-sixth Session of Asam Sahitya Sabha* (Distributed at the Asam Sahitya Sabha session, 9 February 2001).

Brass, Paul R. 1991. *Ethnicity and Nationalism: Theory and Comparison*. New Delhi: SAGE.

————. 1997. *Theft of an Idol: Text and Context in the Representation of Collective Violence*. Calcutta: Seagull.

————. 2003. *The Production of Hindu–Muslim Violence in Contemporary India*. New Delhi: Oxford University Press.

Butalia, Urvashi. 1998. *The Other Side of Silence: Voices from the Partition of India*. New Delhi: Penguin.

Chakrabarty, Bidyut. 2002. "The 'hut' and the 'axe': The 1947 Sylhet Referendum," *The Indian Economic and Social History Review*, 39 (4): 317–50.

Chakraborty, Sanat K. 2000. *Media in Conflict Situation: A Northeast India Perspective*. New Delhi: New Concept Information Systems.

Chakravarti, Uma and Nandita Haksar. 1987. *Delhi Riots: Three Days in the Life of a Nation*. New Delhi: Lancers.

Chaliha, Parag (ed.). 1958. *The Outlook on NEFA*. Jorhat: Asam Sahitya Sabha.

Chamori, S. P. 1993. *Rafting down the Mystic Brahmaputra*. New Delhi: Vikas.

Chanbe, Shibanikinkar. 1973. *Hill Politics in North-East India*. New Delhi: Orient Longman.

Chandra, Bipan. 1971. *Modern India*. New Delhi: National Council of Educational Research and Training.

Chaudhuri, Kalyan. 1994. "Outrage in Assam," *Frontline*, August 26: 28–35.

Chaudhuri, Kalyan. 1998. "The Bloodshed in Assam," *Frontline*, September 26.

Choudhury, D. P. 1978. *The North-East Frontier of India: 1865–1914*. Calcutta: The Asiatic Society.

Choudhury, Paritosh Paul. 2000. *Raktanjalee: Bangla Bhasha Shongramer Itihash* (History of Bengali Language Struggle) (Bengali). Calcutta: Bishodani Prokashoni.

Chowdhury, Prosenjit. 1994. *Socio-Cultural Aspects of Assam in the 19th Century*. New Delhi: Vikas.

Cohen, Abner. 1969. *Customs and Politics in Urban Africa: A Study of Hausa Migrants in Yoruba Towns*. Berkeley, CA: University of California Press.

Cohn, Bernard S. 1987. *An Anthropologist among the Historians and Other Essays*. New Delhi: Oxford University Press.

Daniel, Valentine. 1996. *Charred Lullabies: Chapters in an Anthropography of Violence*. Princeton, NJ: Princeton University Press.

Das, Amiya Kumar. 1982. *Assam's Agony: A Socio-Economic and Political Analysis*. New Delhi: Lancers.

Das, J. N. (1986) "Genesis of Tribal Belts and Blocks of Assam," in B. N. Bordoloi (ed.), *Alienation of Tribal Land and Indebtedness*. Guwahati: Tribal Research Institute.

Das, S. K. 1989. *Spotlight on Assam*. Chanderpur: Premier.

Das, Veena (ed.). 1990. *Mirrors of Violence: Communities, Riots and Survivors in South Asia*. New Delhi: Oxford University Press.

———. 1998. "Specificities: Official Narratives, Rumour, and the Social Production of Hate," *Social Identities*, 4 (1): 109–30.

Das, Veena, Arthur Kleinman, Mamphela Ramphele & Pamela Reynolds (eds). 2000. *Violence and Subjectivity*. Berkeley, CA: University of California Press.

Das, Veena, Arthur Kleinman, Margaret Lock, Mamphela Ramphele & Pamela Reynolds (eds). 2001. *Remaking a World: Violence, Social Suffering, and Recovery*. Berkeley, CA: University of California Press.

Dasgupta, Abhijit. 2000. "The Puzzling Numbers: The Politics of Counting 'Refugees' in West Bengal," *South Asian Refugee Watch*, 2 (2): 64–73.

Dasgupta, Anindita. 2000. "Political Myth-Making in Postcolonial Assam," *Himal*, 13 (8): 14–23.

Datta, P. S. 1993. *Autonomy Movements in Assam (Documents)*, New Delhi: Omsons.

———. 1995. *Ethnic Peace Accords in Assam*. New Delhi: Vikas.

Deka, Meeta. 1996. *Student Movement in Assam*. New Delhi: Vikas.

During, Simon. 1993. *The Cultural Studies Reader* (2nd edn). London: Routledge.

Dutt, Kesav Narayan. 1953. *The Asom Sahitya Sabha: A Brief History of the Association and Its Work*. Shillong: Asom Sahitya Sabha.

Dutta, Narendra Chandra. 1968. *Land Problems and Land Reforms in Assam*. New Delhi: S. Chand.

Engineer, Asghar Ali (ed.). 1984. *Communal Riots in Post-Independence India*. Hyderabad: Sangam Books.

Fenton, Steve. 2003. *Ethnicity*. Cambridge, UK: Polity.

Freitag, Sandria. 1990. *Collective Action and Community: Public Arenas and the Emergence of Communalism in North India*. New Delhi: Oxford University Press.

Fuchs, Martin & Antje Linkenbach. 2003. "Social Movements," in Veena Das (ed.), *The Oxford India Companion to Sociology and Social Anthropology*. Oxford: Oxford University Press.

Gamson, William A. 1988. "A Constructionist Approach to Mass Media and Public Opinion," *Symbolic Interaction*, 11 (2): 161–74.

Gamson, William A. & Andre Modigliani. 1989. "Title of Article," *American Journal of Sociology*, 95 (1): 1–37.

Gellner, Ernest. 1983. *Nations and Nationalism*, Ithaca, NY: Cornell University Press.

———. 1997. *Nationalism*, London: Phoenix.

Ghosh, Partha S. 2001. *Migrants and Refugees in South Asia: Political and Security Dimensions.* Shillong: NEHU Publications.

Glazer, Nathan & Daniel P. Moynihan (ed.). 1963. *Beyond the Melting Pot.* Cambrdige, MA: MIT Press.

Goffman, Ervin. 1975. *Frame Analysis: An Essay on the Organization of Experience.* Harmondsworth, UK: Peregrine Books.

Gohain, Hiren. 1980a. "Cudgel of Chauvinism," *Economic and Political Weekly*, 15 (8): 418–20.

———. 1980b. "Resisting Fascist Trend," *Mainstream*, 18 (31): 28.

———. 1985. *Assam: A Burning Problem.* Guwahati: Spectrum.

Gohain, U. N. (1999/1942). *Assam under the Ahoms.* Guwahati: Spectrum.

Goswami, Atul, Homeswar Goswami, & Anil Saikia. 2002. *Migration to Assam: 1951–1991* (Summary Report of Omeo Kumar Das Institute of Social Change, Guwahati).

Goswami, Priyam. 1999. *Assam in the Nineteenth Century: Industrialization and Colonial Pentration.* Guwahati: Spectrum.

Goswami, Sandhiya. 1997. *Language Politics in Assam.* Delhi: Ajanta.

Goswami, Surendra Kumar. 1986. *A History of Revenue Administration in Assam (1226–1826 A.D.).* Guwahati: Spectrum.

Guha, Amalendu. 1977. *Planter-Raj to Swaraj: Freedom Struggle and Electoral Politics in Assam 1826–1947.* New Delhi: Indian Council of Historical Research.

———. 1980. "Little Nationalism Turned Chauvinist: Assam's Anti-Foreigner Upsurge," *Economic and Political Weekly*, 15 (41–43): 1699–720.

———. 1981. "Little Nationalism Turned Chauvinist: A Reply," *Economic and Political Weekly*, 16 (17): 781–84.

———. 1984. "Nationalism: Pan-Indian and Regional in a Historical Perspective," *Social Scientist*, 12(2): 42–65.

Guha, Ranajit (ed.). 1982a. *Subaltern Studies.* New Delhi: Oxford University Press.

———. 1982b. "On Some Aspects of the Historiography of Colonial India," in Ranajit Guha (ed.), *Subaltern Studies I: Writings on South Asian History and Society.* Oxford: Oxford University Press.

———. 1983a. *Elementary Aspects of Peasant Insurgency in Colonial India.* New Delhi: Oxford Univeristy Press.

——— (ed.). 1983b. *Subaltern Studies II.* New Delhi: Oxford University Press.

——— (ed.). 1984. *Subaltern Studies III.* New Delhi: Oxford University Press.

——— (ed.). 1997. *Subaltern Studies Reader, 1986–1995.* New Delhi: Oxford University Press.

Gupta, Dipankar. 1996. *The Context of Ethnicity: Sikh Identity in a Comparative Perspective.* New Delhi: Oxford University Press.

Gupta, Shekhar. 1984. *Assam: A Valley Divided.* New Delhi: Vikas.

Gupta, Surendra K. & Indira B. Gupta. 1990. *Conflict and Communication: Mass Upsurge in Assam.* New Delhi: Har-Anand.

Halbwachs, Maurice. 1950. *The Collective Memory* (with an introduction by Mary Douglas). New York: Harper Colophon.

———. 1992. *On Collective Memory* (edited and with an introduction by Lewis A. Coser). Chicago: University of Chicago Press.

Hall, John A. (ed.). 1998. *The State of the Nation: Ernest Gellner and the Theory of Nationalism.* Cambridge, UK: Cambridge University Press.

Hansen, Blom. 2001. *Violence in Urban India: Identity Politics, 'Mumbai,' and the Postcolonial City.* Delhi: Permanent Black.

Haqqi, S. A. H. (ed.). 1984. *Democracy, Pluralism and Nation-Building.* Delhi: NBO Publishers.

Hazarika, B. B. 1987. *Political Life in Assam during the Nineteenth Century.* Delhi: Gian.

Hazarika, Sanjoy. 1994. *Strangers of the Mist: Tales of War & Peace from India's Northeast.* New Delhi: Penguin.

———. 2001. *Rites of Passage: Border Crossings, Imagined Homelands, India's East and Bangladesh.* New Delhi: Penguin.

Hechter, Michael. 1986. "A Rational Choice Approach to Race and Ethnic Relations," in D. Mason & J. Rex (eds), *Theories of Race and Ethnic Relations.* Cambridge, UK: Cambridge University Press.

Hirschman, Charles. 1987. "The Meaning and Measurement of Ethnicity in Malaysia: An Analysis of Census Classifications," *The Journal of Asian Studies*, 46 (3): 555–82.

Hobsbawm, Eric. 1990. *Nations and Nationalism since 1780: Programme, Myth, Reality.* Cambridge, UK: Cambridge University Press.

Hobsbawm, Eric & Terence Ranger (eds). 1983. *The Invention of Tradition.* Cambridge, UK: Cambridge University Press.

Horowitz, Donald L. 2001. *The Deadly Ethnic Riot.* New Delhi: Oxford University Press.

Hunter, W. W. 1990/1879. *A Statistical Account of Assam.* Guwahati: Spectrum.

Hussain, Monirul. 1993. *The Assam Movement: Class, Ideology and Identity.* Delhi: Manak.

Hutchinson, John & Anthony D. Smith (eds). 1996. *Ethnicity.* Oxford: Oxford University Press.

Jeffrey, Robin. 2000. *India's Newspaper Revolution: Capitalism, Politics and the Indian-Language Press, 1977–99.* London: Hurst.

Kar, Makhanlal. 1997. *Muslims in Assam Politics.* New Delhi: Vikas.

Karotemprel, Sebastian. 1993. *The Catholic Church in Northeast India 1890–1990.* Shillong: Firma KLM.

Kimura, Makiko. 2003. "Memories of the Massacre: Violence and Collective Identity in the Narratives on the Nellie Incident," *Asian Ethnicity*, 4 (2): 225–29.

Kholar, V. Len. 1995. *Tiwa Matbadi* (Tiwa Dictionary). Guwahati: Tiwa Sahitya Sabha.

Klapper, J. 1960. *The Effects of Mass Communication.* New York: Free Press.

Kleinman, Arthur, Veena Das, & Margaret Lock (eds). 1997. *Social Suffering.* Berkeley, CA: University of California Press.

Kosicki, Gerald M. 1993. "Problems and Opportunities in Agenda-Setting Research," *Journal of Communication*, 43 (2): 100–27.

Kumar, Anand (ed.). 1999. *Nation Building in India: Culture, Power and Society.* New Delhi: Radiant.

Lijphart, Arend. 1996. "The Puzzle of Indian Democracy: A Consociational Interpretation," *American Political Science Review*, 90 (2): 258–68.

Mahajan, Gurpeet (ed.). 1998. *Democracy, Difference and Social Justice.* New Delhi: Oxford University Press.

Mander, Harsh. 2008. "Nellie: India's Forgotten Massacre," *The Hindu*, December 14, 2008.

McClain, Paula D. (ed.). 1993. *Minority Group Influence: Agenda Setting, Formulation, and Public Policy*. Westport, CT: Greenwood Press.

McCombs, Maxwell E. & Donald L. Shaw. 1972. "The Agenda-Setting Function of Mass Media," *Public Opinion Quarterly*, 36 (2): 176–87.

M'Cosh, John. 1986/1837. *Topography of Assam*. New Delhi: Logos.

Mehta Commission Report. 1985. *Report of the Non-Official Judicial Inquiry Commission on the Holocaust of Assam Before, During, and After Election, 1983*. Guwahati: Asom Rajyik Freedom Fighters' Association.

Miri, Sujata. 1993. *Communalism in Assam: A Civilizational Approach*. Delhi: Har-Anand.

Misra, Udayon. 1981. "Little Nationalism Turned Chauvinist: A Comment," *Economic and Political Weekly*, 16 (8): 290–92.

———. 1999. "Immigration and Identity Transformation in Assam," *Economic and Political Weekly*, 34 (21): 1264–71.

———. 2000. *The Periphery Strikes Back: Challenges to the Nation-State in Assam and Nagaland*. Shimla: Indian Institute of Advanced Study.

———. 2001. *The Transformation of Assamese Identity: A Historical Survey*. Shillong: North East India History Association.

Moore, P. H. 1997/1910. *Autumn Leaves from Assam*. Guwahati: Spectrum.

Morley, David & Kuan-Hsing Chen (eds). 1996. *Stuart Hall: Critical Dialogue in Cultural Studies*. London: Routledge.

Mukherji, Partha N. 1994. "The Indian State in Crisis? Nationalism and Nation-Building," *Sociological Bulletin*, 43 (1): 21–49.

Moscovici, S. 1985. *The Age of the Crowd: A Historical Treatise on Mass Psychology*. Cambridge, UK: Cambridge University Press.

Nag, Sajal. 1990. *Roots of Ethnic Conflict: Nationality Question in North-East India*. New Delhi: Manohar.

Narayan, Hemendra. 2008. *25 Years on…Nellie Still Haunts*. Delhi: Shilpayan.

Neog, Maheswar. 1976. *The Annals of Asam Sahitya Sabha*. Jorhat: Asam Sahitya Sabha.

———. 1984. "Assam Agitates Against Foreign Nationals," in B. L. Abbi (ed.), *Northeast Region: Problems and Prospects of Development*, pp. 275–86. Chandigarh: Centre for Research in Rural and Industrial Development.

Oommen, T. K. 1988. "Nation, State and Ethnicity: Towards a Conceptual Clarification," *Social Action*, 38 (4): 333–43.

———. 1990. *State and Society in India: Studies in Nation-Building*. New Delhi: SAGE.

———. 1995. *Alien Concepts and South Asian Reality: Responses and Reformulations*. New Delhi: SAGE.

———. 1997. *Citizenship, Nationality and Ethnicity*. Cambridge, UK: Polity Press.

———. 2002. *Pluralism, Equality and Identity: Comparative Studies*. Oxford: Oxford University Press.

Pan, Zhongdang & Gerald M. Kosicki. 1993. "Framing Analysis: An Approach to News Discourse," *Political Communication*, 10 (1): 55–75.

Pandey, Gyanendra. 1982. "Peasant Revolt and Indian Nationalism: The Peasant Movement in Awadh, 1919–1922," in Ranajit Guha (ed.), *Subaltern Studies I*, pp. 143–97. Oxford: Oxford University Press.

Pandey, Gyanendra. 1992. "In Defense of the Fragment: Writing about Hindu–Muslim Riots in India Today," *Representations*, 37 (Special Issue, Winter): 27–55.

———. 1994. "The Prose of Otherness," in David Arnold and David Hardiman (eds), *Subaltern Studies VIII*, pp. 188–221. Oxford: Oxford University Press.

———. 2001. *Remembering Partition: Violence, Nationalism and History in India*. Cambridge, UK: Cambridge University Press.

———. 2006. *The Construction of Communalism in Colonial North India* (2nd edn). New Delhi: Oxford University Press.

Pardesi, Ghanshyam. 1980. "Exploitation and Alienation: Assamese View," *Mainstream*, 18 (30): 9–10.

People's Union for Civil Liberties (PUCL) Team. 1980. "The Magnitude of Assam Disorder," *Mainstream*, 18 (28): 18–21.

Phadnis, Urmila. 1989. *Ethnicity and Nation-building in South Asia*. New Delhi: SAGE.

Phukon, Girin. 1996. *Politics of Regionalism in Northeast India*. Guwahati: Spectrum.

Phukan, Girin & N. L. Dutta (eds). 1997. *Politics of Identity and Nation-Building in North-East India*. Dibrugarh: Dibrugarh University.

Plummer, Ken. 1983. *Documents of Life*. London: George Allen & Unwin.

Rajagopal, Arvind. 2001. *Politics after Television: Hindu Nationalism and the Reshaping of the Public in India*. Cambridge, UK: Cambridge University Press.

Rehman, Teresa. 2006. "Nellie Revisited: The Horror's Nagging Shadow," *Tehelka*, September 30.

———. 2009. "An Untold Shame," *Tehelka*, March 14.

Rao, V. Venkata. 1976. *A Century of Tribal Politics in North-East India, 1874–1974*. New Delhi: S. Chand.

Reddi, P. S. 1984. "Genesis of the Assam Movement", in B. L. Abbi (ed.), *Northeast Region: Problems and Prospects of Development*, pp. 259–66. Chandigarh: Centre for Research in Rural and Industrial Development.

Reid, Sir Robert. 1997/1942. *History of the Frontier Areas Bordering on Assam from 1883–1941*. Guwahati: Spectrum.

Roudometof, Victor. 2002. *Collective Memory, National Identity, and Ethnic Conflict: Greece, Bulgaria, and the Macedonian Question*. Westport, CT: Praeger.

Roy, Beth. 1994. *Some Trouble with Cows: Making Sense of Social Conflict*. New Delhi: Vistaar.

Saikia, Rajen. 2000. *Social and Economic History of Assam (1853–1921)*. New Delhi: Manohar.

Saikia, Yasmin. 2004. *Assam and India: Fragmented Memories, Cultural Identity, and the Tai-Ahom Struggle*. Delhi: Permanent Black.

Sarkar, Radha Kanta. 2000. *Assam—Heritage and Anarchy*. Calcutta: Bharati.

Sarkar, Sumit. 1983. *Modern India, 1885–1947*. New Delhi: Macmillan.

Sarmah, Alaka. 1999. *Immigration and Assam Politics*. Delhi: Ajanta.

Scheufele, Dietram A. 1999. "Framing as a Theory of Media Effects," *Journal of Communication*, 49 (1): 103–22.

Sen, Sipra. 1999. *Tribes and Castes of Assam: Anthropology and Sociology*. New Delhi: Gyan.

Sen, Swagata. 2006. "Nellie Massacre in Assam (Review of 'Come What May' by Arun Shourie)," *India Today*, December 18, 2006.

Sharma, S. L. & T. K. Oommen (eds). 2000. *Nation and National Identity in South Asia*. Hyderabad: Orient Longman.

Sharma Thakur, G. C. (1986) "Land Alienation and Indebtedness in the ITDP Areas of Assam: A Case Study of Marigaon ITDP," in B. N. Bordoloi (ed.), *Alienation of Tribal Land and Indebtedness*, pp. 101–11. Guwahati: Tribal Research Institute, Assam.

Shourie, Arun. 1983. "Come What May," *India Today*, May 15.

Singh, B. P. 1987. *The Problem of Change: A Study of North-East India*. Oxford: Oxford University Press.

Singh, Jaswant. 1984. "Assam's Crisis of Citizenship: An Examination of Political Errors," *Asian Survey*, 24 (10): 1056–68.

Skaria, Ajay. 1999. *Hybrid Histories: Forests, Frontiers and Wildness in Western India*. Oxford: Oxford University Press.

Smith, Anthony D. 1991. *National Identity*. Harmondsworth, UK: Penguin.

Spencer, Jonathan. 2003. "Collective Violence" in Veena Das (ed.), *The Oxford India Companion to Sociology and Social Anthropology*. Oxford: Oxford University Press.

Sword, Victor Hugo. 1992/1935. *Baptists in Assam: A Century of Missionary Service, 1836–1936*. Guwahati: Spectrum.

Takeshita Toshirō. 1998. *Media no Gidai Settei Kinō: Masukomi Kōka Kenkyū ni okeru Riron to Jisshō*. Tokyo: Gakubunsha.

Talukdar, Sushanta. 2005. "Violence in the Hills," *Frontline*, November 5.

———. 2007. "Migrants' massacre," *Frontline*, January 13.

———. 2008. "Communal Inferno," *Frontline*, November 7.

Tambiah, Stanley J. 1996. *Leveling Crowds: Ethnonationalist Conflicts and Collective Violence in South Asia*. New Delhi: Vistaar.

Tan, Tai Yong & Ganesh Kudaisya. 2000. *The Aftermath of Partition in South Asia*. London: Routledge.

Thompson, E. P. 1971. "The Moral Economy of the English Crowd in the Eighteenth Century," *Past and Present*, 50 (1): 76–126.

Thompson, Paul. 1978. *The Voice of the Past: Oral History*. Oxford: Oxford University Press.

Tilly, Charles. 1978. *From Mobilization to Revolution*. New York: Random House.

Trivedi, V. R. 1995a. *Documents on Assam: Part A*. New Delhi: Omsons.

———. 1995b. *Documents on Assam: Part B*. New Delhi: Omsons.

Varshney, Ashutosh. 2002. *Ethnic Conflict and Civic Life: Hindus and Muslims in India*. New Delhi: Oxford University Press.

Weiner, Myron. 1978. *Sons of the Soil*. Princeton, NJ: Princeton University Press.

———. 1983. "The Political Demography of Assam's Anti-Immigrant Movement," *Population and Development Review*, 9 (2): 279–92.

Wilcox, R. (1998/1832–33). *Memoir of a Survey of Assam and the Neighbouring Countries: Executed in 1825–6–7–8*. Calcutta: R. N. Bhattacharya.

Wilkinson, Steve Ian. 2000. "India, Consociational Theory, and Ethnic Violence," *Asian Survey*, 49 (5): 767–91.

———. 2004. *Votes and Violence: Electoral Competition and Communal Riots in India*. Cambridge, UK: Cambridge University Press.

Wilson, Jane S. 1992. "Turmoil in Assam," *Studies in Conflict and Terrorism*, 15 (4): 279–92.

B. Debates on the Antiforeigner Movement in Assam in the Economic and Political Weekly (1979–81)

Date	Title	Author	Pages
1979.01.13	Great Nationalism, Little Nationalism and Problem of Integration: A Tentative View	Amalendu Guha	455–58
1980.02.23	Cudgel of Chauvinism	Hiren Gohain	418–20
1980.03.15	Assam: Cudgel of Chauvinism or Tangled Nationality Question?	Sanjib Kumar Baruah	543–45
1980.03.22	Letters to Editor: Assamese People Agitation	Gail Omvedt	580
1980.03.22	Assam: Fall-Out of Underdevelopment	Hiren Gohain	589–90
1980.03.29	Letters to Editor: Ganging Up against the Left	P. C. Mathur	621
1980.04.19	Assam–1: Worse than Emergency Day	Udayon Misra	731–32
1980.04.19	Assam–2: Tangled Theories	Hiren Gohain	733–35
1980.04.19	Assam–3: Two Refugee Camps and an 'Unpatriotic' Journalist		735
1980.05.10	Assam and Delhi	Romesh Thapar	835
1980.05.10	Immigration and Demographic Transformation of Assam, 1891–1981	Susanta Krishna Dass	850–59
1980.05.17	Assam–1: Beyond Patriots and Traitors	Sanjib Kumar Baruah	876–78
1980.05.17	Assam–2: Incidents in North Kamrup	Nirupama Bargohain	878
1980.05.17	Assam–3: Another View of Incidents in North Kamrup	Vibhuti Patel	879
1980.06.07	Assam–1: Varieties of Alienation		997–98
1980.06.07	Assam–2: Internal Colony in a National Exploitative System	Ghanshyam Pardesi	1001–2
1980.06.14–21	Assam: Communal Bloodletting	Correspondent	1036
1980.06.14–21	Assam: Left in Waiting	Yogi Aggarwal	1046–47
1980.08.02	Assam: Fresh Tension in Upper Assam Tea Belt	Udayon Misra	1300–1301
1980.08.02	The Assam Question: A Historical Perspective	K. M. Sharma	1321–24
1980.08.09	Assam: Tangle Jargonized	Hiren Gohain	1337–38
1980.08.09	Assam: A Colonial Hinterland	Tilottoma Misra	1357–64

Date	Title	Author	Pages
1980.08.16	Assam: Union Bashing	Seema Guha	1388–89
1980.10.25	Little Nationalism Turned Chauvinist: Assam's Anti-Foreigner Upsurge	Amalendu Guha	1699–720
1980.12.06	The Assam Question: A Historical Perspective A Comment	Lily Bara	2063–64
1981.02.21	Assam: National Register of Citizens, 1951	Anil Roychoudhury	267–68
1981.02.21	Little Nationalism Turned Chauvinist: A Comment	Udayon Misra	290–92
1981.02.28	Little Nationalism Turned Chauvinist: A Comment	Hiren Gohain	339–40
1981.03.28	Little Nationalism Turned Chauvinist: A Comment	Gail Omvedt	589–90
1981.04.11	Little Nationalism Turned Chauvinist: A Comment	Sanjib Kumar Baruah	676–80
1981.04.25	Little Nationalism Turned Chauvinist: A Reply	Amalendu Guha	781–84
1981.05.16	Little Nationalism Turned Chauvinist	Hiren Gohain	924
1981.05.23	Assam's Industrial Development: Urgency of New Direction	Atul Goswami	953–56
1981.05.23	Little Nationalism Turned Chauvinist: A Summing Up	Amalendu Guha	957–64

Index

riots, 1, 2
   in Gujarat and Delhi, 3
   against Muslim immigrants, 9
   Tiwa villagers, 14
riots, to interpret
   agency of rioters, 29–34
   collective violence and party politics, 26–29
   Colombo riots, 1983, 22–24
   communal riots and colonialism, 24–26
   Delhi riots, 1984, 22–24
   violence and identity, memory of, 34–37
Roy, Beth, 31
rural communities, 113n20

Samajwadi party, 141
"satyagraha," 68
Sharma Thakur, G. C., 53
Shourie, Arun, 83
Singh, Manmohan, 136, 141
Sixth Schedule of Constitution of India, 128
social memory, 35
social movements, 6
"sons of the soil" movement in Assam, 10
spontaneous phenomena, 20
State Legislative Assembly, 34
State Legislative Assembly election, 85, 136
Subaltern Studies Group, 30, 78

Tetelia Tribal Block, 103
Tewary, T. P., 83
Tewary Commission Report, 73, 84, 136, 143
Theft of an Idol, 27
The Production of Hindu-Muslim Violence in Contemporary India (Brass, 2003), 27

Thompson, E. P., 30
Tiwas
   autonomous movement, 128
   leadership of AASU, 121–22
   movement for autonomy, 115, 127–28
   and Muslim immigrants, 130
Tiwa villagers
   peasants of rural areas, 6–7
   riots, 14
tribal block, 95
tribalism, 25
tribal land alienation, 123–24
tribal massacre, 1

"Udayachal," 75
ULFA's Assamese nationalism, 145
United People's Front (UPF), 128
UPF. *See* United People's Front

Varshney, Ashutosh, 28
violence
   communal, 1
   ethnic and communal identities, 9
   memory and, 13–15, 115–16
   routinization of, 3
Vishwa Hindu Parishad, 31

Weiner, Myron, 55–59, 61
Wilkinson, Ian, 28

Xaxa, Virginius, 113n19
xenophobic movements, 5

zamindari system, 95

About the Author

Makiko Kimura studied at the Jawaharlal Nehru University (New Delhi) for her PhD degree. She was a postdoctoral research fellow (2004–2007) of the Japan Society for Promotion of Science and research associate (2007–2011) at the International Peace Research Institute, Meiji Gakuin University (Tokyo). She is an associate professor at the Tsuda College (Tokyo) and teaches transnational sociology. She engages herself in activism supporting indigenous rights movement. She lives in Japan.